THE VINYL CAFE
NOTEBOOKS

ALSO BY STUART McLEAN

FICTION

Stories from the Vinyl Cafe

Home from the Vinyl Cafe

Vinyl Cafe Unplugged

Vinyl Cafe Diaries

Dave Cooks the Turkey

Secrets from the Vinyl Cafe

Extreme Vinyl Cafe

NON-FICTION

The Morningside World of Stuart McLean

Welcome Home: Travels in Small-Town Canada

EDITED BY STUART McLEAN

When We Were Young:
An Anthology of Canadian Stories

STUART McLEAN

THE VINYL CAFE NOTEBOOKS

VIKING
CANADA

VIKING CANADA

Published by the Penguin Group

Penguin Group (Canada), 90 Eglinton Avenue East, Suite 700,
Toronto, Ontario, Canada M4P 2Y3 (a division of Pearson Canada Inc.)

Penguin Group (USA) Inc., 375 Hudson Street, New York, New York 10014, U.S.A.
Penguin Books Ltd, 80 Strand, London WC2R 0RL, England
Penguin Ireland, 25 St Stephen's Green, Dublin 2, Ireland (a division of Penguin Books Ltd)
Penguin Group (Australia), 250 Camberwell Road, Camberwell, Victoria 3124, Australia
(a division of Pearson Australia Group Pty Ltd)
Penguin Books India Pvt Ltd, 11 Community Centre, Panchsheel Park,
New Delhi – 110 017, India
Penguin Group (NZ), 67 Apollo Drive, Rosedale, North Shore 0632, New Zealand
(a division of Pearson New Zealand Ltd)
Penguin Books (South Africa) (Pty) Ltd, 24 Sturdee Avenue, Rosebank,
Johannesburg 2196, South Africa

Penguin Books Ltd, Registered Offices: 80 Strand, London WC2R 0RL, England

First published 2010

1 2 3 4 5 6 7 8 9 10 (RRD)

Copyright © Stuart McLean, 2010

Illustration of crow copyright © Dan Page, 2010

The Vinyl Cafe is a registered trademark.

Manufactured in the U.S.A.

Library and Archives Canada Cataloguing in Publication data available
upon request to the publisher.

ISBN: 978-0-670-06473-1

Visit *The Vinyl Cafe* website at **www.vinylcafe.com**

Visit the Penguin Group (Canada) website at **www.penguin.ca**

Special and corporate bulk purchase rates available; please see
www.penguin.ca/corporatesales or call 1-800-810-3104, ext. 2477 or 2474

For CBC Radio,
for giving me a place
to do what I love

All that I hope to say in books,
all that I ever hope to say,
is that I love the world
E.B.WHITE

CONTENTS

CALENDAR NOTES

NOTES FROM THE NEIGHBOURHOOD

TASTING NOTES

READER'S NOTES

NOTES FROM THE ROAD

NOTES TO SELF

 NOTES

FROM HOME

DRIVING THE 401

My dear friend,

I am on the road again. Just a short trip to Montreal and back. We left home yesterday morning and drove along the 401 in an old tour bus that Blue Rodeo used last week in the Maritimes. Our tour manager, Don, set off from London at eight in the morning and picked me up at ten in a shopping mall parking lot by the highway. We picked up Bill, who is doing the sound at tonight's show, at a roadside hamburger joint in Port Hope.

Don and Bill are in the back of the bus watching a video as I write. I am alone in the front. I have Steel Rail on the surround sound stereo, cranked up loud. They are on the show today. You would enjoy them, I think. I am listening to them sing about the highway right now. While I listen, I am watching the highway slip by, and writing this note to you.

So many times we have made this trip together. You and I. I remember the time the snow began almost the moment we left. It didn't look serious at first. It was blowing in fine wisps across the top of the pavement.

I said, "I bet that is the way sand blows across the desert at the start of a windstorm."

By the time we got to Belleville, the snow was hitting the windshield on the horizontal and I was peering over the wheel. All that was left of the pavement was two black stripes. I wonder if you remember that trip? It was a long time ago. Come to think of it, I'm not sure we had even met. That drive was with someone else. I don't think you would have liked it, though. There were hundreds of cars in the ditch. Hundreds! Cars were flying off the road all around us. It was as though someone were sweeping them away. I wanted to stop, but the person I was with, the one I thought might have been you, insisted we keep going. It took thirteen hours to cover what will take us five hours to cover today. God willing.

I remember another trip. This one was in the summer. I still had the old Toyota. It didn't have air conditioning, and the gear box, which was right between the two front seats, used to heat that car up like an oven. I was driving with my boys, who were still young at the time. We stopped every half-hour for Popsicles and pop or I swear we would have passed out.

Everyone says the 401 between Montreal and Toronto is the most boring stretch of highway in the country. I guess they are right, but it holds a lot of memories for me. That is for sure.

I have driven it more times than I care to remember. I have stopped at the Big Apple for pie, and at Iroquois to watch the ships slip through the lock. I have driven in the morning, and I have driven at night, in search of love, and away from love, and back to love. I was born in Montreal, but these days I live in Toronto. That means no matter which way I am going, whether I am driving from east to west, or west to east, I am both leaving home and coming home.

I used to believe the getting there was the important thing. Now it's good enough just to keep moving.

Anyway. It has been forever since we have spoken. That is my fault. And I apologize. And I hope you understand. I am doing the best I can. I will try to do better when I get home.

The sign we passed says we are almost in Napanee. That means we are almost halfway home. No matter which way we are heading.

3 March 2002

THE PIANO

I was seven years old the afternoon I had my first piano lesson. My teacher was a young man from Scotland. His name was Mr. McLachlan. He wore tweed sports jackets and carried a soft leather briefcase, and, like the doctor and the bread man and the milkman back in those unhurried days of the mid-1950s, he came to the house.

Mr. McLachlan came once a week: Wednesday afternoons after school. He and I would go down to the basement, past the furnace and into the playroom my father had finished with blue-stained plywood and tiles. There was a blackboard on one wall, and a pretty good train set, and in the corner, an old upright piano.

The piano wasn't there for the early lessons. At the beginning Mr. McLachlan taught, and I practised, on a fold-out cardboard keyboard. Eventually the upright piano arrived, and that, as you might imagine, was a big deal. Especially after the cardboard keyboard.

The piano in the basement was where Mr. McLachlan and I did our work. Or, more to the point, didn't. Even back then, when I was still in the single digits, I was capable of disappointing and well aware of the disappointment I was causing

Mr. McLachlan. Despite my mother's encouragement, I never brought discipline or attention to my practising. The two things that were, really, the only requirements for forward motion.

Oh, I progressed. I wasn't hopeless. My right hand conquered the treble clef in a boyish way, but my left hand lumbered around the bass notes without any confidence, like a dim cousin trying to find his way along a crowded street, always stopping to stare at the street signs myopically and falling behind everyone else.

How Mr. McLachlan kept coming week after week, year after year, is beyond me. He must have had a pupil somewhere who made it worthwhile. Whoever it was, probably some studious girl, it certainly wasn't me.

And so it was that my piano lessons eventually, and thankfully, ended. Mr. McLachlan and I were put out of our pain.

My brother took lessons too. And probably my sister; I don't remember about her, but we all stopped. The years slipped by, and somehow I ended up with the piano—probably because I took guitar lessons at university, probably because I became the writer. I was the artsy one. I was also closest to the piano. My brother and sister lived on the other side of the country.

The first place it went was in the living room of my first apartment. I remember how, reunited, I took renewed interest in it; sadly, my self-discipline and perseverance, not to mention my talent, hadn't developed over the years. Not surprisingly, neither had my playing.

When I married, the piano came with me into my new home, and when I had children of my own, they took piano lessons too. I used to sit with them while they practised, and sometimes we soared over it, and sometimes we fought over it, and when all was said and done, they had more success than I, for sure, but not *much* more success. Not meaningfully more. They grew up, and left home, and sadly I did too, and the piano came with me again.

We have been through a lot together, this piano and I. A lot of years if nothing else, close to half a century.

And a year ago I bought a new house. It is a modest place, and there is no room for a piano in my new house, unless I wanted to have a living room without a sofa. Or an office without a desk. And I decided I didn't.

My problem, as moving day approached, was what to do about the piano. Selling it, the reasonable thing to do, seemed out of the question. I couldn't bring myself to do it.

I decided I would lend it to someone. They could have it until, well, until I needed it back. Where and when and why that might be I had no idea, but when I did find someone who thought they might be interested, I assured them it wouldn't be anytime soon.

You would think there would be lots of takers. There was only one, and they had it for about a year. Then one day they phoned me and said, "We made a mistake, we want to give you your piano back. There's no room here either."

And so I did the only thing I could think of doing. I arranged to have my piano placed in storage.

And that is where it is today. Although, as I say that, I realize I have no idea whatsoever exactly *where* that is. I haven't visited the piano, or even asked about it. It is just away, somewhere. It costs $50 a month to keep it there.

I am assuming that because the people who are looking after it are in the business of doing this, storing pianos, that they have given it a good home, and my fifty bucks is buying decent accommodations. I am assuming that it isn't sitting in someone's backyard under a tarp. But that's an assumption; I don't *know* that.

I imagine it to be in an old warehouse. An old brick-walled factory dating back to the 1920s, where they once manufactured electric fans, or corn brooms, and today is just a room where someone works on pianos. My piano, and a few others like mine, are lined up against the brick wall. I like to think that at night, when the piano tuners have gone home, and the lone security guard has fallen asleep at his post, people appear to play these pianos. Men and women living in cramped apartment buildings, who long to play but haven't the space or resources for a piano. Or maybe the spirits of all the players from the past who find the temptation of one last concert too much to pass up. And they sit and play the music I never could while the moonlight streaks through the warehouse windows. But that's just fantasy. I know my piano is just sitting there, under its storage blanket, and that every month I pay to keep it there is another month that it is unplayed.

So this is what I want to know. Why am I holding on to it? Why can't I say goodbye?

Am I honouring memories here? My father? Who is ninety years old now and built that room in the basement and got the piano down there. Not negligible things. Mr. McLachlan? My boyhood? All those years—can I sell them? Can I give them away for nothing? Am I holding on to a road to the past? There are, I've noticed, fewer and fewer.

Or is it a road to the future? Do I think that one day, one of my sons is going to show up, like I did, and say, "Where is that piano, anyway?" Do I think I have to hold on to the past so I can pass it on to the future? So what, if when they asked, I said, "I sold that piano." Would that really matter?

Or are we talking about dreams here? Do I, in my disorganized and busy little imagination, believe that one day I will call up the people at the warehouse and say, "I want my piano back, bring it home"? Am I, stuck in my fifties, still dreaming that one day I will do away with the desk, or the sofa, roll up my sleeves and sit down the way my mother and Mr. McLachlan always wanted me to, and apply myself to the mathematical mysteries of the key of C?

Is this what happens to dreams? Do they all end up in brick warehouses? And you pay people $50 a month and they look after them for you? It costs $50 a month to keep them free from rain, or sleet, or snow, until the day you phone and say, "I'm ready now; bring me my dream." And they put it in a truck, and they bring it to your house, and as they carry it down the stairs to the room that you have made for it especially—*your little dream*—you think to yourself, *This time I am going to practise every day. This time, it is going to work out.*

15 April 2007

MY PALM TREE

I was living in a modest home at the time. Not, frankly, the kind of home where you would expect to find a palm tree. Then one Sunday afternoon, unexpectedly, I bought myself another. House, that is. The new house came first. The palm tree came later. But the two events are all part and parcel. The palm wouldn't exist without the house. Or not in my life, anyway.

This is what happened.

A real estate agent, a friend of mine, phoned and said she had seen a house that she thought I would like.

"I am not in the market for a new house," I said.

"I think you should come and see it," she repeated. "I think you would like it."

So I went. The moment I saw it, I knew I was doomed. It was the house I had wanted all my life. I *had* to own it, and there was no time to dither. If I was going to get this house, I had to make an offer then and there. So that is what I did, and it was accepted, and there I was at bedtime faced with the terrifying prospect of owning two homes. I had to sell the one I was living in, the one that had been, up until that Sunday afternoon, perfectly acceptable but now no longer was. And I had to sell it fast.

The real estate agent who had lured me into this predicament agreed, reluctantly, to handle the sale.

"We are going to have to fix this place up if we are going to have any hope of selling it," she said, wrinkling her nose in distaste.

By "we" she meant "me."

She put me in touch with a man whose job it is to make disreputable houses irresistible. One of the things the man did was stand in my living room and point at the window where my desk was.

"Get rid of that desk," he said. "Move the couch. Buy a palm tree."

I got rid of the desk and moved the couch, but I decided that a palm tree, which I suspected would cost a couple of hundred dollars, was excessive. I decided not to get the palm.

A week passed. A couple of weeks passed. And then a month. My house didn't sell. Then one day, when I was at the local corner store, the kind of place where you go for a pack of cigarettes or a lottery ticket but certainly not a palm tree, I saw they had a palm for sale: $125.

I explained my housing predicament to the man behind the counter. I asked if he would consider renting me the palm.

"I just live around the corner," I said. "I just need it for a week or two."

I promised to be careful with his palm. I offered him $25 rent, and the opportunity to sell it once I was finished with it. This didn't seem as good an idea to him as it did to me. He showed me another palm, a less robust palm.

"Fifty bucks," he said.

So I bought a palm tree. And wouldn't you know it, my house sold.

Not knowing what else to do with it, and feeling a certain obligation, I took the palm with me to my new house.

I am not one of those people who are good with plants. In fact, until I bought the palm, I didn't own any houseplants. Not one.

Don't get me wrong. I like green things. From time to time I buy cut flowers. But I am not good with them either. Even cut flowers seem to die faster in my care than they do in the care of others. But their death never feels like a tragedy. Or, more to the point, like it is my fault. Cut flowers are, after all, supposed to die. It is the natural order of things. The death of a vase of tulips is like the passing of an elderly aunt— something to mourn, perhaps, but not to fret over. The death of a house plant always feels more like a homicide. Or at least manslaughter. I have stayed away from them.

But suddenly, as well as my new house, I owned a plant— the palm—and because we had been through something together, I felt this obligation.

I can't say for sure that my palm *was* the reason my house sold. But I can't say it wasn't either. It did look spectacular by the window where the desk used to be.

And now, a year has passed, and I have cared for my palm, if not religiously, at least responsibly. Enough, anyway, that it is still alive. I feel good about that.

I have learned a number of things about and from it. I have learned that when it wants to grow a new frond, it shoots out a spearlike appendage that stands around for weeks, somewhat stiffly, like an awkward guest at a cocktail party, until one day, *abruptly and for no apparent reason*, it unfolds. I have learned that when the current fronds turn brown, and my palm appears to be dying, and I feel like giving up on it, I shouldn't. Because if I keep watering it and cut off the old growth, new growth appears. So far, anyway. The lessons I have learned from it are the important lessons of patience and faith.

I don't want to give you the idea that I am the perfect owner. I am not the perfect owner. My palm doesn't look as good today as it did when I got it. But let's be honest, neither do I.

My palm tree is, after all, clearly out of place in the city where I live, a little tropical tree cast ashore in the cold north, first finding refuge at a corner store of all places and then in *my* home. I don't know which would be worse. We have endured, my palm and I, and now we are heading toward our second winter together.

The way of the heart is often a mystery. It is hard to know why we love the things we love. And maybe it is better that way. But I do know this. We grow to love the things we care for. We like the responsibility, I think. It feels good to be needed.

I am now a guy with a new house and a palm tree. I don't want my little tree to be homeless again. I want us to make it through this winter. Together.

15 November 2009

LOSING PAUL

It was late afternoon. I was sitting at my desk. The phone rang. I looked up at the name and the number on the call display and my stomach lurched. I thought, *Why is Alan phoning me from Moncton?*

Alan and I hadn't spoken for years. Not that we had had a falling out. Just that we had been busy, living our lives. I didn't want to pick the phone up. I did, of course.

"Alan," I said, picking up *too* quickly. "How are you?"

"Not good," he said.

The next part came out rushed.

Alan said, "We lost Paul."

Or maybe he said, *Paul's gone.* Then his voice cracked, and he didn't say anything else.

It was my turn. And I can't remember what I said. Probably I said, *Oh no.* Or maybe, *What happened?* Or maybe I swore. Probably all three.

Paul and I met, long ago and far away, at a summer camp in the Laurentian Mountains. We were students; working at camp was our summer job. We worked together for three summers and went to the same university.

At school, we shared a student apartment—a basement

place so small and dingy that the rent was $25 each a month. Paul's brother, Alan, who was phoning from Moncton to tell me Paul had died, lived in that apartment too.

There were two bedrooms. We flipped a coin, and Alan won. So Paul and I shared the remaining bedroom. It was so small we had to build a set of bunk beds.

"It was cancer," Alan said. "It started in his lungs. By the time they found it, it had moved to his bones."

They thought he would live until the spring. But that morning, the morning of the telephone call, his wife, Kathy, couldn't wake him. He just stopped breathing.

I drove to Peterborough for the funeral. I went with a friend who didn't know him but who came so I didn't have to go alone. We arrived just as the service was starting. We had to sit in the balcony of the church. I didn't think I was going to cry, but I did.

The minister quoted Emily Dickinson in her homily. "Parting," wrote Dickinson, "is all we know of heaven, and all we need of hell."

Death is always a surprise, even when it isn't. And it always comes with grief. My grief for Paul is coloured by this: I let him slip away from me.

My dear, good friend Paul, whom I used to play squash with, and drink beer with, and who loved canoeing, and recommended books that I should read, slipped away as we grew up and got busy with our lives. He slipped away, and now he is gone, and I am left with the worst of all the emotions. I am left with regret. Deep regret.

I was in Peterborough, where Paul lived, not two months ago. And when I was there, I thought, *I should call Paul.*

Sometimes I phoned him when I was there, but I didn't phone him on that visit because I was busy and tired and whatever. And now I have been kicking myself all over the place.

I went back to his house after the funeral. Kathy gave me a hug.

"I can't tell you how many times I thought of phoning you these last six months," she said.

The house was crowded. I found Paul's daughter in the kitchen. The kitchen of a house I had never been in.

"Have you seen your picture?" she asked me.

It was stuck on a corkboard by the phone, an old passport picture, taken when I was in my twenties. My hair is long and curly. I have no idea how Paul got it.

"How long has this been here?" I asked.

"As long as I can remember," said Paul's daughter. "It's been there all my life."

Clearly I was still in Paul's heart too. But he hadn't been phoning me either.

Alan told me that when Paul found out he was sick he asked his brother to let me know. Alan couldn't explain why he hadn't called. But I understand. Who wants to make that kind of call? That's the kind of call you put off. And I understand why Kathy didn't phone either.

I feel sad they didn't, because I would have visited. But it wasn't Kathy and Alan who messed up. It was Paul and me.

If we had been doing our job, the sorrow I am feeling today would have been the deep sorrow that comes with parting, not the pain of regret.

15 January 2006

WATCHFULNESS

I have a garden this year.

It is not, as gardens go, either a big or an ambitious garden. Just a swath of black earth that runs along the back fence, the width of my modest backyard, that, until this spring, I allowed the weeds to have their way with.

I would have let them have their way with it again this summer except for some ambitious friends who took pity on me and my backyard and arrived one evening with shovels and other gardening stuff and got it going. They brought some irises from their garden and some shrubs from Canadian Tire and a trillium they had dug up from the woods, which they hinted might be illegal. (I am doing my best to look after it, and it seems to be doing fine, and certainly getting more water than it would in the woods.)

And lo and behold, inspired by their industry, I added a plant myself. A plant I bought on a whim at IKEA, which I thought should get some wild time. It seems happy out there, nestled in the shade, not far from the trillium.

And that should have been that, but there were still some empty spaces, so last weekend I went to a nursery and bought tomato plants, which I put in pots, and they are thriving, and herbs (the ones you would expect) and a Brussels sprout vine, because I *like* Brussels sprouts and it amuses me to think I might grow my very own, and then as I was leaving, I thought, *I should get some flowers too.*

Well, I had never bought flowers in a nursery before, so I bought the only ones I knew. I bought a flat of morning glory—those soft and moon-shaped flowers that open and close so wondrously every morning, and go on and on all the way to October.

I am pleased by all the activity, and how good it all looks, but what interests me about this is not how I have worked on my little garden, but how my little garden has worked on me.

It has made me watchful.

Every morning before breakfast, I stand on my deck with my mug of tea and watch it, checking out how things are doing in the kingdom of dirt.

At noon I watch again, and in the evenings too. Mostly I am watching the tomatoes, and the morning glory in their glorious run up the back fence, wondering, as I watch, if it can be truly possible that I will get red fruit and blue flowers where once all I got were weeds.

Other things I have been watching since my garden began instructing me are the other residents of my backyard, the birds—a red-winged blackbird, some warblers, a house finch and more sparrows than you can shake a stick at—and the hungry squirrels, who have become my mortal enemy.

All of this watchfulness in the natural world has got me watching other things as well. I've been watching, for example, the stain on the bottom of my freezer more intently. It appeared there the day I left the freezer open, or as I would rather we referred to it, during the great spring thaw. It is a deep purple stain, richer and redder than the iris, but browner than the tomatoes. And I know I should get in there and clean it, but that would involve removing the freezer drawers, something I am unsure can be done, so in the meantime I am simply watching. And I can report that the stain, unlike the trillium, is not growing at all.

I am also watching my weight, and trying to watch my health, and I have been meaning to dig out my kite and take it down to Cherry Beach and watch it for a while too.

While I am at it, I can also tell you I have *not* been watching the Stanley Cup Playoffs, *So You Think You Can Dance*, the television news or, sadly, over you.

Which I would be happy to do if you would call when you weren't in such a hurry to get to wherever it is you are going today.

So I am not watching over you, not today, but will be soon enough, I hope. In the meantime the morning glory will have to do.

3 June 2007

MY "TO DO" LIST

I am at loose ends. To be honest, I am at a complete loss.

Somehow, somewhere, sometime since I went to bed last night and woke this morning, my "to do" list went missing.

I know you are thinking I misplaced it. But not so. I wouldn't misplace something as important as my "to do" list. I suspect it was tidied up.

It was written in dark blue ink on a piece of yellow lined paper. And when I say *it,* I don't want you to think that there was only one item on my list and that I should be able to remember it. There was way more than one item.

I can't possibly remember everything on the list. That's why I had a list.

Yes, I know. I am always putting my glasses down somewhere that I can't remember. This is different. This is my list of things to do. And no, I don't remember where I was when I had it last. Please don't ask me that again.

I don't know what I am meant to be doing, and it is making me agitated.

Are you sure you haven't seen it? Let me tell you what it looks like. There was actually more than one list. There were several lists, each in different quadrants of the page: things to do, people to write, people to call.

And there was a little doodle in the top right corner: a picture of a hammer smashing a little animal that you might mistake for a squirrel but is actually the neighbour's dog (who wouldn't stop yapping when I was working on my list).

I keep thinking of the people on my list. Were you on my list?

Are you someone sitting in a coffee shop waiting for me? Are you a dentist standing beside an empty dentist chair, dentist tools laid out beside you? I am not coming.

If there is a paucity of me where you are, and there shouldn't be, if there should be more of me than there is, it is not personal.

You might have heard already. I lost my list of things to do.

I want to assure you that I am going to begin a new list. I have already, actually. But you aren't on it yet. So far there is only one item on my new list. Number one—find missing "to do" list.

Which is why I am talking to you now.

If by any chance you have my "to do" list, could you please call me? If you don't have my number, you could phone any of the numbers on the list and ask them for my number. Tell them I said it's okay for them to give it to you. I'll come and pick the list up.

It suddenly occurs to me that someone *other* than you might have the list.

Was I supposed to call you today? Has someone else already called? Have you received any confusing phone calls?

It is possible my list has fallen into the hands of one of those people who like to get things done. One of those people who, unlike you and me, actually enjoys sitting down and crossing things off lists.

Maybe someone like that found my list in their pocket. And no, I don't have any idea how it got there. But if it did, and if she is one of those people who like getting things done, maybe she was delighted to reach into her pocket this morning and find my list, with all those things just begging to be crossed off.

If you are the person who has my list and are getting my things done, I appreciate that, but I would appreciate it more if you would just return my list to me, because you aren't doing these things for me. You are doing them for yourself. And you should get your own list, because I am beginning to feel unhinged without mine.

And though I understand how you may be feeling smug about getting all those things done, have you stopped to think what it is like being me? Not having the vaguest idea of what you are supposed to be doing?

Just give it back.

I live in the house with all the windows beside the one with the little yappy dog that is starting to drive me crazy. Honest to God, when are they going to take that dog inside and feed it?

Where is my list? I want my list back.

You can have my glasses. And my keys. And my cellphone and all the other things I've lost. Just give me the list. And then you can do whatever you want to the dog.

I will look after the dog right now if you will just *give me the list.*

Listen to me. Do you know what would happen if I don't do the things I am supposed to do? If I stop calling and writing and showing up? If I unplug?

You don't have to answer that.

Okay, I warned you.

I'm over it now.

It's gone. Do what you want with it. I don't need it anymore. I am done with "to do" lists. I am beginning again. I am starting fresh. I am going upstairs to write out a list of things I don't have to do.

You can have my "to do" list. I am starting my "to don't" list.

And I don't care what happens to it.

18 January 2009

ANTS

I have had, for longer than I can say with certainty—more than a few days or weeks, but not years, so for a certain number of months that I have not kept track of—a solitary ant on patrol in my upstairs bathroom. Always one, never more, often in the sink, but not always in the sink. Sometimes on the counter.

I say *on patrol*, but I don't know that. I have no idea if my ant is there with any purpose in mind. I just know he is there every time I go into the bathroom, or almost every time, so he is clearly not just passing through. He could be on guard, but on guard for what, I can't imagine. He could be a spy. He could be there for any number of things really, including because he is thirsty.

I can't say much about him with any certainty, except that he is almost always there. I don't even know if, in fact, he *is* just one ant, or one in an ever-changing number of ants. A revolution of ants.

I don't even know if it is biologically possible that he is, or has been, the same ant all these months, because my lack of knowledge when it comes to ants is almost complete, and includes a lack of knowledge regarding the life expectancy of ants.

If I had to guess, I would say they live for a season. Although exactly what a season is where ants are concerned is beyond me. And surely these chilly January days are not that. Ant season, I mean. Yet, if I were to get up right now, and we were to go to my bathroom, we would find it is ant season there. Or it is for my ant. Because if we were to do that now, check out my bathroom, we would almost certainly find him.

I say *he* when actually I know one thing about this ant. He, it turns out, is a *she*.

I have been reading up on ants and have learned they are almost always *shes*. If there is work to be done, it turns out, women do the work in the world of ants. The men are there for the purpose of procreation and then they take off.

Anyway, as I said, if she *is* working, I am not sure exactly *what* she is working at.

There *was* a time when I *might* have known this. If this was a Victorian January for instance, I probably *would* have known this. Victorians are renowned for their knowledge of the natural world. They would talk about these things at dinner parties: about their latest birdwatching trip, or their collections of curiosities, feathers and eggs, whatever. It was part of the Victorian tradition to study and observe nature. We don't do that so much anymore.

I think 2008 was the year when, for the first time in history, more people lived in cities than they did in the countryside. We city folk are more intent on poisoning ants than observing them.

Little surprise then that most biologists agree that we are in the middle of the Sixth Great Extinction. There have been five already, according to our understanding of fossils. The last one was the extinction that took out the dinosaurs, and a lot of other things as well.

And while you get the feeling there will be ants around long after ... well, long after any of us are worrying about ants, and that ants probably don't need anyone's help, least of all mine, it did occur to me that the ants in my bathroom might be looking for a hand. It might not be the best time of the year for them to be up and about, and maybe they have been marching around my bathroom looking for something to eat. *Scavenging* is what the biologists would call it. So I got a little honey and mixed it with water and put out the honey water on the counter beside a small piece of tuna, and I sat down to see what would happen. And lo and behold, within ten minutes, my solitary ant had been joined by five of her sisters. They drank the honey water, but they seemed to like the tuna best.

And you don't have to write me, telling me that it is a crazy thing to do, to feed ants. It may be crazy but no crazier than a lot of things I do. As far as I can see, these ants mean no harm to me. And I don't mind sharing the odd teaspoon of protein. There is enough for all of us in my house. So I have *kept* feeding them, and I have been watching them, and I have almost figured out where they come from. I suspect that if I keep watching, and even follow along, there is no telling where they might lead me.

23 January 2010

KEEPSAKES

I have a small wooden bowl on my bedroom bureau. It is made of Norway pine. My uncle Hugh turned the bowl in his workshop when he lived on Flinders Island, off the southeast coast of Australia. I knew him by reputation only. I met him once, but that was when I was a boy. I know only that he was an architect, and a sailor, and that he lived in Melbourne, Australia, until he retired to Flinders Island, where he made my bowl.

I keep the bowl on my bureau because it is my connection to him. And through him, in a way I cannot fully explain, to my father's boyhood, an event that happened in that faraway country and, therefore, an event that has always been far away from me.

We hold on to these things—photographs, old sweaters, jewellery, small bowls—in the hope that they will whisper a secret password, the door to memory will blow open and we'll find ourselves alone, with all our little memories lined up and tagged, and stamped, and stickered, just for us.

Some come to us as birthrights, some as legacies of love. Some of them lead to a notch in our heart so plain that any fool could see it, there like a scratch across a dining room table or paint splashed on the kitchen floor.

Sometimes they lead us to memories so faint that we don't even know we have them. Memories that haunt our hearts like watermarks, and we have to hold our hearts up to the light, and get the angle just right, because the memory isn't really our memory, and we're not sure how it got there, only that it lingers in our heart, the way smoke lingers in our hair after we have stood close to a fire.

These are the ciphers of memory, and when we find them we know they are trying to point us to something important, even if we can't untangle the meaning. All we know is that this thing we are holding is an important thing, and we should cherish and protect it.

There is a small wooden bowl on my bureau. It is made of Norway pine.

2 February 2000

THE SENTIMENTALITY OF SUITS

I was rummaging in a rarely visited corner of my closet when I came across my blue blazer. The moment I saw it, I was overtaken by a compulsion to put it on. I am wearing it now, as I sit writing, a little overdressed for a guy who won't be leaving the house today: black jeans, a dress shirt and the blazer. Though in a private nod to my casual impulses, I have left the dress shirt untucked.

I haven't worn the blazer for at least a decade. There is nothing wrong with it. In fact, as blazers go, it is a nice one: a pure wool Polo blazer, by Ralph Lauren, with a fetching red-and-black pinstriped silk lining.

I bought it when I worked, briefly, in television, which means it is at least twenty-five years old. But it is a classic design and not unstylish all these years later, especially with the jeans and the untucked shirt.

I have a long history with blazers. As a child, I went to a boys' school where we all wore them.

A blue blazer, grey flannel pants and a white shirt and tie is a good look for a boy. Unfortunately, I carried the look with me into adulthood. A grown man in grey flannels and blazer looks like a poetry teacher at an English prep school. It took me a while, but I now understand that this is not a good look for an adult, which is why the blazer was in the back of my closet. My question is, Why have I held on to it? For decades?

First, I would put forward, because of the sentimental attachment. I have had a blazer in my closet, or thrown over my bedroom chair, pretty much since I was eleven years old. I am not sure what might happen if I didn't have one. Something bad, probably.

I own other articles of clothing like this, clothes that I never wear anymore but feel attached to nonetheless. There is a brown corduroy jacket, for instance, that isn't, but looks just like, the brown corduroy jacket that my first-ever girlfriend, Joanne, made for me. How can I throw it away? It's a stand-in, yes, but it stands in my closet as a symbol of young love. And speaking of love, there is also the suit I was married in. I bought it, on a Friday night, in between flights, at Brooks Brothers in Boston. Racing to the store from the airport in a taxi, I bought the entire wedding kit in no time flat: a white shirt, a muted tie and the dark blue suit.

I had tried to buy a wedding suit before I left home. My friend Suanne still tells the story of how I called from a downtown men's store, stuffed, pathetically, into a sleek Italian suit.

"Come and tell me if it is all right," I begged.

Suanne jumped into a taxi. "Holt Renfrew," she barked. "It's an emergency."

When she got there, she looked at me and sniggered. "It looks like that suit is wearing you," she said.

By the time I hit Boston, I was suit-less and just one flight away from my own wedding. I was desperate, and therefore flushed with both pride and relief when I got the job done.

Pleased as punch that I had pulled it off, and with time to kill before my plane, I wandered down Clarendon Street and, eventually, into another men's store, a stylish place called Simon's, where a flamboyant young salesman took me under his wing, poured me a glass of ouzo and asked me to show him what I had bought. He took one look at the shirt and tie I had chosen and wrinkled his nose.

"Is this a wedding? Or a funeral?" he asked. "Are you happy about this?"

It didn't take much for him to talk me into a happy shirt and an exuberant red tie that I was almost too shy to wear.

The shirt long ago vanished, and the lining on the tie is gone, and, sadly, I am no longer married, but the suit is still in my closet, hanging there loyally, with the conviction I lost. And though, perhaps appropriately, it doesn't fit me anymore, it is a silent reminder of a great good thing, and it is not going out. Not ever. It has a lifetime membership, and I have packed and unpacked it each time I have moved, with a tinge of melancholy but never regret.

There are other things like it. A shirt that was once in style but isn't anymore. I don't wear it either, but I did to great effect for a while.

"Look at you," said a pretty girl one night. "That is a stylish shirt."

There is a velvet jacket that I bought from a vintage store, that I could once pull off but wouldn't try to these days. And other stuff too.

There is part of me that believes if I threw any of these things out, or dumped them in a Goodwill box, it would be daring the world to turn on me. You think you are too good for that blazer, Mr. Fancy Pants? Well, deal with this then. And there would be a huge economic conflagration, and I would lose my job, and the ability to pay for power and, more importantly, heat, and I would be huddled in my basement freezing. And if I only hadn't thrown out the blazer, and all those sweaters, at least I wouldn't be so cold.

But it is more than that. There is also my apprehension that if I were to throw the blazer out, blazers would immediately come storming back into style. Everyone would be wearing blazers, and I would have to go out and buy another one, and every time I put on my new blazer, I would be consumed by self-loathing for having thrown out the perfectly good one.

Part of it is crazy, and part of it is utilitarian, but most of it is sentiment. The sentimentality of my suits. My wistful and sad-eyed connection to cloth and to the memories and moments from my past that are worn into the knees and the elbows. The things that were, and the things that could have been. The rips in my sweaters, the holes in my heart.

3 April 2009

THE MORNING PAPER

Newspapers have always been a big part of my life. When I was a boy we subscribed to two. We would read the morning paper at the breakfast table. My dad got the front section. My brother and I fought over sports and comics. If there was time, we traded sections.

Our second paper came in the afternoon. This was in the 1950s, when there still were afternoon papers. It seems quaint now, like a second mail delivery. We had those too, a service left over from the days when writing a letter was the most efficient way to get a message across town. Catch the morning post for the afternoon delivery. *Please come to supper.*

Anyway, our second newspaper arrived, like a dinner guest, just before dinner. And when it did, the family would gather in the living room and read it. My father would sit in the same chair every night and, whisky in hand, offer a mumbled commentary on what he was reading. There were lots of crooks in my father's paper. He always found plenty of stories to confirm the opinion, which he expressed at night, but never lived by, that the world was full of liars, crooks and cheaters.

My paper was different. My paper was filled with enticing ads for films I was too young to see, stories about heroic hockey players and want ads with an endless list of things for sale that I was desperate to own. *Pets for Sale* was my favourite section. I followed *Pets for Sale* with the intensity with which I follow political affairs today. And of course, the advice columns: Ann Landers in the morning and her more restrained twin sister, Abby, at night.

At the end of the day, after supper, we would wrap the day up the way we began it, with the newspaper. Every day we used that day's paper to wrap our garbage. Plastic garbage bags had yet to be invented. So in those days you wrapped your garbage in newspaper and dropped it in your steel garbage cans.

Garbage was my father's job. He tackled the garbage after he tackled the dishes, which in retrospect he should get credit for. That was a long time before even Ann Landers was advocating that sort of manly contribution to household affairs.

The point is that our days were bracketed in newsprint. It came *in* the front door by morning and went *out* the back door by night.

Even when I crawled into bed, I took the newspaper with me. Instead of reading the adventures of the Hardy Boys, like everyone else I knew, I travelled in the world of Ken Holt— the son of a globe-trotting foreign correspondent and a newspaper boy himself. Ken and his buddy Sandy Allen, he of the newspaper-owning Allen family, were my heroes.

And now, some fifty years later, little has changed. I have managed to find my way to one of the only cities on the continent with one, two, three, four daily newspapers. I subscribe to one, buy the others from time to time, and have a fifth, *The Guardian Weekly*—a summary of *Le Monde, The Washington Post, The Observer* and, of course, *The Guardian*—mailed to me once a week.

I have lived my life with newsprint.

I love my work on the radio, but it could have been otherwise. Just out of college, I was offered a job by the feisty and crusading newspaperwoman Margaret "Ma" Murray. I saw her interviewed on television during a political convention, and I was smitten. So when I graduated, I hitchhiked across the country from my home in Montreal to the interior of British Columbia, to the town of Lillooet in the Fraser River Canyon, where Murray ran *The Bridge River-Lillooet News*. She was in her eighties at the time and had announced her imminent retirement. I went to offer her my services.

"You don't want to retire," I told her. "You want to slow down. If you hire me, we can make it work. Together."

Honest to God, I said that.

She took me home and fed me lunch, and then, wonder of wonders, she offered me a job. Minimum wage, no overtime. I was inexperienced, wet behind the ears and stunned.

"I have to go home and think about this," I said.

She said, "You'll need some sustenance for the road. I'll make you a sandwich." She picked up a chicken breast, bone and all, from the bowl on the table and slammed it between two pieces of bread.

"Here," she said, holding it out.

It was the last time I saw her. I started hitchhiking home and, a few days later, frozen and ignored on the edge of the highway in the middle of a miserable November rainstorm in the middle of British Columbia, I gave up the ghost, left the highway and climbed on a train.

There was a girl involved. I missed her. When I got home, I was offered another job, and I chickened out on Lillooet.

And so ended my newspaper career. I have often wondered what might have happened if I had thrown caution to the wind. I know one thing for sure: I would have been one of those reporters who hung around the press room. And by that I don't mean the news room. I mean around the presses. Twenty years later, when I was a young man married to a different girl and working for the CBC, whenever I got a late-night twitch for news (this was in the years before you could surf the net), I would head down to *The Globe and Mail* press room on Front Street around midnight and snatch a copy of the next morning's paper before I went to bed. You can't do that anymore. Or I can't. They have moved the presses to the suburbs.

Newspapers got me going. And I have made my way, or most of it anyway, as a journalist. But I have never been a newspaperman. I don't think I have ever had anything published in a newspaper, not even a letter to the editor. Nevertheless, newspapers have been a constant in my life, and if I hadn't stumbled into CBC Radio, they might well have *been* my life.

I love newspapers. I love getting up in the morning and opening the front door and finding one on my stoop. I have never seen the guy who delivers it. I have no idea who he is. But I trust him, and he has never failed me.

I love the gestalt of the front page. I love carrying the paper to the table and reading it while I wake up.

And later in the day if I find myself alone with nothing to do and feeling anxious because of it—say I am meeting someone in a restaurant for lunch, and I arrive first—whereas other people might buy a drink and settle down to wait, I start looking for a paper. They calm me. They reassure me. They make me feel safe and sound.

There is much to recommend newspapers. Others have written about these things better than I, so I will not repeat them.

But I would like to say two things. The first is that I like newspapers because they exist in space, but not in time. They happen out of time. In fact, they literally *stop* time. Every day the newspaper jams its wrench in the cogs of the clock and says, *This is what it is like right now.* And by doing that, it asks the same of all of us. It asks us to step out of time too and consider the things that are happening and what they might mean to us and to others. It asks us what we think about all that.

The second thing, and perhaps the most important thing, is that a newspaper is a shared experience. On every level. Not only the shared experience of a boy listening to his father grumble about the news. Or two brothers squabbling over the sections. There is all that, but there is more.

When our cities are full of newspapers, they are, quite literally, on every corner. You don't even have to read them to know what they are on about. You just have to walk around and they will seep into you like ink spilled on a blotter, and in the spilling, they will stain your mind. And that means we are all ink-stained—those of us who read the papers, and those of us who don't. We are stained with the same stories, and because of that, all of us, living together, can carry on a common conversation.

And this act of *sharing the experience* is arguably as important as the experience itself. More important, maybe. For it is in the sharing that we foster fellowship. And *that* is what creates community. If everyone has their own private newspaper, as the webmasters would have it, we *may* all be as well informed, quite possibly better informed, but we will become a society of solitudes, each of us lost in our private prejudices. And rather than argue with each other over what might and might not be the common good, we will drift away to the islands of the single issues and soon be lost in the forests of alienation. And soon enough, instead of grumbling at the paper, we will be grumbling at one another, and engagement in the world of politics will seem meaningless to us. Why even vote?

When we all read the same newspapers, it means we are all on the same page. When we don't, group activities become personal activities, the great public conversation ceases, and before we know it, we are bowling alone.

A newspaper is a grand public space, and all these grand technologies that would replace it—cellphones and laptops, iPods and iPads—take public spaces and turn them into private spaces. The net, with all its weblike connectivity, is still essentially a private place. One person with a search capacity. Each of us a webmaster assembling our own personal narrative.

And in our excitement with it all, and dear God don't think I am not excited too, we think we can abandon papers to no effect. That it is just another summer evening, and we can throw them out with the recycling.

What I am trying to say here is that our newspapers are more than the sum of their parts.

And I know, I know, you don't have to say it. I am slashing at waves with my sword. But take note: at the same time that our newspapers are folding, so are our broadcasters.

We have to keep the public conversation going.

My father is now ninety-two. It was, I think, Bette Davis who said, "Old age is no place for sissies." At ninety-two my father has given up a lot. But he hasn't given up his newspaper. It still comes every morning. His paper, *The Montreal Gazette*, began publishing in 1785. It was started by a printer named Fleury Mesplet, who came to Montreal with Benjamin Franklin when the army of the American Revolution invaded and occupied the city of my birth. When the revolutionaries came, they dragged a printing press with them from Philadelphia. The first in the city. The idea was that Mesplet would start a newspaper that might convince Canadians to join the Revolution. Franklin and the revolutionary army eventually left town. Mesplet stayed.

My father still gets the paper Mesplet began. He no longer reads it every day, but he keeps his subscription. We, his family, worry that if it stops coming altogether it would be at his peril. While the paper is there, beside his chair, he is still ink-stained, still part of the conversation, still grumbling.

3 April 2009

RADIO

I have loved radio as long as I can remember—even as a young boy, radio seemed like a magic thing to me. I was the perfect audience: awkward, unsure and without a community of my own. The world of radio was a world where I could belong, a place where I was just as good as everyone else. Listening to the radio, alone in my bedroom, gave me a sense of connection to the larger world.

Montreal was a great city to begin a radio romance. It was a radio hothouse, with Paul Reid personifying the elegance of CJAD, Gord Sinclair Junior, the scrappiness of CFCF, and Joe Pyne summing up CKGM. Pyne was the wooden-legged firebrand who more or less invented the call-in show. Before he hung up on them, he regularly invited his callers to gargle with razor blades.

My favourite Joe Pyne story, though it has never been verified to my knowledge, involves the night he supposedly insulted Frank Zappa.

"I guess your long hair makes you a woman," crowed Pyne at his guest.

"And I guess your wooden leg makes you a table," Zappa allegedly shot back.

True or not, if you remember Joe Pyne, you will know that that transaction sounds like it might have happened. It pretty much sums up his show. I couldn't get enough.

The first radio I remember was a white plastic Fleetwood we kept on the breakfast table. Eventually the Fleetwood was upgraded, and on one of the greatest days of my life, I was allowed to take it upstairs to my room and set it on the night table beside my bed. Because it was a tube radio, it would warm up and glow like a flashlight running on low batteries— a comforting thing to have beside you on a winter's night. Lying in bed listening to Dave Boxer on CFCF, or Joey Reynolds on WKBW, was like lying beside a campfire that could talk.

One night, when I was listening to Danny Gallivan chant the holy passage of a Montreal Canadiens hockey game, I responded to the cheeriness of the radio by inviting it to join me under the covers—I probably thought it would keep me warm. The light from the tubes was even prettier under the covers, and I was so comfy, snuggled up beside it, that I fell asleep, and pretty soon it got so hot that the plastic body started to melt. By all rights I should have gone up in smoke. The only reason I didn't is that my father was seized by his own impulse that night, an impulse he was never able to explain. Uncharacteristically, he came upstairs to check on me.

I guess he saved my life, and I guess it was inevitable that I would end up working in radio—seeing as how I was sleeping with them before I hit puberty.

6 June 2010

PETER GZOWSKI

Peter Gzowski died on Thursday. We knew it was coming. I spent the early part of the week sitting in my office staring at the walls. Before the tributes began, it was a week of waiting. Today, I just feel sad and lonely.

Peter had a remarkable career. He did great work. Somewhere, a long time ago, he decided it was his mission to uncover the best of Canada, the people and the places, to seek them out and introduce them to the rest of us.

Because he decided this was important work, and because he was so good at it, we believed it was important work too and we went along for the ride. Somewhere along the way, Peter became what he was looking for. He became a part of the best of Canada.

He was the best of CBC Radio, that is for sure.

He was a sort of quilt maker. The individual parts of his quilt were often ordinary. Some of the moments, of course, were extra special: the first interview with Ellie Dansker and the Red River Rally, to name two. But mostly, like any quilter worth their salt, he worked with scraps. It was only when you stepped back and looked at the overall effect that you realized the grandeur of his creation.

People are always asking me what he was like. He was a bundle of contradictions. He wasn't the guy you thought you knew from the radio. And he was the guy you knew from the radio.

If you didn't know him, and you met him, you might have been disappointed. You might have thought he was chilly and standoffish. He wasn't chilly and standoffish. But he acted that way sometimes. People say he was shy. I think he was more private than shy. I think there is a difference.

He was certainly complicated.

He was a man who dealt in the realm of ideas. But he was driven to ideas by instinct and emotion. He was the Canadian nationalist who, more than anything, wanted to have written for *The New Yorker* magazine.

He was a serious person who liked to play games—especially if they involved words. He was sloppy about his clothes and meticulous about his grammar.

On New Year's Eve, this year, he provoked one of the guests he had invited for dinner to search through a stack of reference books in an effort to determine whether it was more Canadian to say *railroad* or *railway*.

He was more a journalist than a gentleman.

He was thoughtful and he was selfish.

His work absorbed him. He noticed everything—except the world around him. One day, his friend Peter Sibbald Brown went over to Gzowski's cottage at Lake Simcoe. You didn't knock on the door up there, you just wandered in, so Peter Sibbald Brown wandered in and found the cottage filled with smoke—coughing, eye-stinging smoke, and he thought to himself, *Even Gzowski couldn't generate this much smoke.* He put his hands over his eyes, and staggered in, and found a log had tumbled out of the fireplace and was smouldering away on the hardwood floor.

Gzowski was sitting at his computer in the little alcove where he worked. He had noticed the smoke. But his offhanded response was to crack the window open about a quarter of an inch.

That is how I will remember him, at work in a smoke-filled room. Sitting across from me, perhaps, in a radio studio, with just minutes before we go to air, his head is down, he is ignoring me. He is using a black felt marker to scribble a last-minute note onto his script, rewriting his intro fifteen seconds before we're on. Just before the control room gives us the go-ahead, he looks up at me with a mischievous smile. That's how I will remember him.

He grinned like that on the radio, and in his home—pleased as punch whenever he found a question that would shift the spotlight off him. His mission was to make the other shine brighter. He seemed to bring out the best from those he was with.

I will remember him in the early morning at Lake Simcoe, sitting at the end of his dining room table, bare feet, absorbed by the crossword, a cup of coffee going cold beside him, his fingers, already in the early morning, ink-stained. I'll remember him looking up with that twinkle and bringing something up from the night before. And while you were busy thinking about that, he will ask your opinion about some political issue that is bothering him and you know absolutely nothing about, leaving you standing there wondering whether you should fess up or fake it.

He loved to laugh.

And because I loved him, I loved to make him laugh.

Over a period of about a decade, I had a regular spot on his radio show, *Morningside*. Of all the things we did together, his favourite was the day we cracked up. I was in the middle of an inconsequential item, and we both got the giggles, and then fell into out-of-control, gut-sucking laughter. Laughter so wrenching that we couldn't carry on. On the tape of that morning, you can hear us going over the edge and then his desperate attempt to bring us back. We both thought we had crossed some sort of line we shouldn't have crossed. We felt self-conscious about it until the mail started arriving, and we realized quite the opposite. Everyone listening had joined in the laughter.

That's what he did best. He sat in his studio, and he let us join him.

27 January 2002

THE PEOPLE
YOU LOVE

I met him at a wedding. He was about my age. He was a strong, charismatic and intelligent man. We sat beside each other during dinner and then, when the dancing began, we sat and talked. We talked about our children. Eventually he told me about his daughter, Kathy.

Kathy was, he said, his *perfect* daughter—the kind of girl who did well in school, and was quiet, obedient, thoughtful and a delight to be around.

"Perfect, really," he said, until she turned thirteen and started to misbehave. She stopped coming home at a reasonable time. She began to tell lies about where she had been. When she was pushed, she offered excuses instead of the truth—thin ones at that.

The man and his wife soon enough came to understand why their daughter was lying to them. She was going to raves. She was taking drugs. She was hanging out with inappropriate boys, including drug dealers. She was misbehaving in all sorts of ways. Doing things they never dreamed possible. Suddenly his perfect little girl was a disaster. And *he* was terrified.

"Completely terrified," he told me.

I asked him what he did.

"I panicked," he said.

His instincts told him he should make rules. He said he thought if he made enough rules, if he created enough structure, he could pull his daughter out of this mess. It didn't work.

He made rules, *she* broke them. Things got horrible.

At curfew time, my friend would find himself alone in his living room, staring out his living room window at a dark and empty street, pacing around his house with his heart pounding, convinced that he was never going to see his daughter again.

Other nights, he and his wife would get in their car and go looking for her.

"There we were," he told me, "at one, two, three, in the morning, driving aimlessly around searching for our kid."

They wanted to find her. They were petrified that if they did, they would find her beaten unconscious, drugged out or dead. She had immersed herself in a world of criminals, of danger, of tragedy, and one that neither my friend nor his wife had any idea how to navigate.

To make things worse, he and his wife began to fight—bitterly.

"Of course we did," he said. "Our daughter was the most important thing in the world to us. We couldn't agree about what we should do. Nothing we tried worked."

They made an appointment to see a psychologist—someone who came highly recommended. They told their daughter they were doing this. She agreed to come with them, just once, to see what it was like.

The psychologist told them that their daughter was in

trouble. She said that their daughter needed rules and structure. Tough love, the psychologist called it.

Then she said, "You have to get yourself ready to lock her
out if that moment comes. And it will almost certainly come."

When the appointment was over, the man and his wife
walked out of the room. They looked at each other, and one
of them said, "That is just not us."

The doctor's advice struck them as cruel. They couldn't do
any of it. They agreed about that. They didn't *know* the
answer, but it felt as if the doctor were asking them to treat
their daughter as an object, rather than a human, a human
who seemed to need something and was striking out blindly.

They went to see another psychologist. The man described
him as an extraordinary human being. He said it twice.

"Extraordinary."

All three of them went. The psychologist met with them
separately, the man's daughter first. She had agreed, once
again, that she would go that once.

The psychologist talked to Kathy alone, and then he sent
Kathy out and called the man and his wife in.

He said, "I will see your daughter. She is full of big
questions and she is having trouble with all of them. I will see
her, though I don't have much hope that I will be able to help
her."

Then he said, "I think I can help you."

"What?" said the man.

The possibility that *he* might need help had never occurred
to the man.

"What you have to understand," said the psychologist, "is
that your daughter doesn't feel loved."

"But I love her deeply," said the man.

"Listen carefully," said the psychologist. "You may love her, but she doesn't *feel* loved. And she doesn't hear it when you tell her. It doesn't get through to her."

"What should I do?" said the man.

"There are two things you have to do," said the psychologist. "First, you have to keep her at home. Don't put her into the position where she might stay out all night. Young kids can die on the street.

"Make curfews if you want to. But know that she won't keep them. And don't lock her out. She is going through a horrible thing. Let her do it at home where she is safe.

"The second thing you have to do is to communicate to her that she *is* loved. You have to *praise* her, and tell her you *love* her. And you have to do this *over and over and over again*. And you have to do it for a long, long time."

"How can I do *that*?" said the man. "She's sneaking around, and she's lying, and she's doing terrible things. There is *nothing* for us to praise."

"Find something," said the psychologist. "Don't criticize her. Praise her. And do it as often as you can. Eventually she may hear you."

The man looked at the doctor earnestly.

"What," he asked, "if I can't find anything to praise?"

The psychologist looked back at him.

"Fake it," he said.

None of this made sense to the man.

"I thought it was ridiculous," he said.

He went home thinking he was going to make some rules. And he did. And again, nothing changed.

Left with nothing else to try, he decided to try what the psychologist had suggested. But he couldn't find anything that he could praise about his daughter.

"So I lied," he said. "I said things like, 'Your hair looks nice.' Though it didn't. And, 'What a nice wallet.'"

The more he did it, the more the psychologist's prescription began to make sense to him. If his daughter didn't feel loved at home, it would make sense that she would look for love elsewhere. Maybe she had found a community that accepted her no matter how strange she was, or thought she was.

"It was amazing to me," said the man, "that she couldn't see herself as either loved or lovable. It was like she had a perceptual distortion."

So he began. And nothing happened. But he kept it up—for days, and weeks, and months.

And then, things started getting better. Not right away, not even slowly. Slower than slowly. It was a year maybe. After a year, Kathy started doing things that the man actually *could* praise.

"It worked," he said.

It took almost two years. But it worked.

Kathy went to university. She got a bachelor's degree. She graduated on the dean's list and the honour role as well. Now she is in graduate school.

"She grew up to be a kind, sensitive person," said the man.

Then he shook his head and said, "God, it was so hard. She would bring people home. One night she brought a guy home in a blue bunny suit. I hated this guy instinctively. But I didn't say anything."

During the two hard years between the beginning and the end, Kathy saw the therapist irregularly.

The man said, "If you asked her, she would tell you that she doesn't think it helped her in the least. She would also say that the things we did weren't helpful either."

"Maybe that is the case," said the man. "Maybe all that stuff was only helpful to us. Maybe it just helped give us an understanding of what was going on and a framework that enabled us, at the very least, not to hurt her. It certainly made the day-by-day living easier. We avoided all the confrontations that we couldn't win."

Without the intervention of the doctor, the man is sure what he would have been doing.

"I would have been drawing lines in the sand," he said. "And she would have been defiant. We avoided all that."

The man said when all this was happening, he didn't talk about it much.

"You feel lost, and embarrassed, and guilty, and frightened when your child is in trouble."

I know there are people who might be reading this who are in the place that the man was in many years ago. If you are that person, if you are a parent who is afraid, and worried, and feeling alone, he would tell you that you aren't alone. He would tell you that now is the time for you to talk to others. Now is the time to look for help. He would tell you that you do not have to be embarrassed or ashamed.

And if you aren't a parent but are a kid who is doing things that you know aren't right and aren't good for you, it's your time to find someone too. It is time for you to believe, as Max Ehrmann said, that "you are a child of the universe, no less than the trees and the stars; you have a right to be here. With all its sham, and drudgery, and broken dreams, it is still a beautiful world."

There are people waiting to love you. You might not believe that, but that may be the truest thing I have ever written. If they aren't around you now, believe me, they exist. You have a job too. Go and find them.

27 September 2009

CALENDAR NOTES

SIGNS OF SPRING

It was midday. I was at my desk, working at something and listening to Jimi Hendrix. The sun, which was coming through the east-facing window, was shining directly into my eyes. For almost six months the sun had been too low in the sky to do that. I shifted into the shade and kept my head down. A few minutes later, I had to shift again. And after a few more minutes, a third time. I had now shifted so far that I was sitting a full arm's length from my keyboard. Typing was getting increasingly difficult. I pulled myself closer to my desk and attempted to peck away with one hand on the keyboard and the other shading my eyes. After fifteen minutes, I decided I was going to have to deal with the sun if I was going to get any work done.

I would have closed the blind if there was a blind on the window. But there is not a blind on the window. I went in search of the next best thing—a hat.

I had seen a ball cap with a good peak a day or two earlier. That would have done the job, but I couldn't remember where I had seen it. The only hat I could find was an old sou'wester—a black, oiled, broad-brimmed fisherman's hat that I bought in Lunenburg, Nova Scotia, years ago. I have, to my children's great embarrassment, worn it while walking the dog on wet November nights.

I was alone. There was no one to embarrass, so I slipped the hat on and went back into my chair. It turned out to be just the thing. I finished the piece I was working on. Shaded.

Outside in the garden, barely visible, the daffodils have begun their long climb back from their subterranean slumber; across the street, an early robin hops across a neighbour's lawn. Inside, a writer huddles over his keyboard wearing a sailor's storm hat to ward off the sun. The signs of spring are building.

15 April 2007

MAPLE SYRUP TIME

All this week, when Glenn Hodgins gets up in the morning, he has put on a pair of jeans, and then, before he heads outside, he has put on another pair of jeans *over* the first pair. Glenn has a maple bush in Hemmingford, Quebec. March is sugaring season.

Hemmingford is forty-eight kilometres south of Montreal and was at the epicentre of the great ice storm of 1998. Glenn lost hundreds of maple trees in the storm, and this changed the ecology of his sugar bush. The canopy, he says, is thinner than it used to be, which means more light reaches the ground. That is good news if you're a hawthorn or a thimbleberry, but bad news if your job happens to be tapping maples.

"The thimbleberry bushes," says Glenn, "are about seven feet high this year." That's seven feet of thorns.

Glenn says walking through them is painful even when you're wearing two pairs of jeans.

"They cut the jeans to shreds," he says. To protect his hands, Glenn has to wear thick leather gloves even on warm days.

There have been so *many* warm days this winter that some

of Glenn's neighbours have been sugaring through January and February.

"One neighbour boiled twelve hundred gallons of syrup last month," says Glenn.

Glenn is a traditionalist. Glenn sugars by the calendar, and that means the first three weeks of March. So Glenn has been spending the last week fighting through the thimbleberries with a battery strapped on his back, wearing a drill in a holster, with his pockets full of tools and splices, cutters and hose clamps.

Glenn gathered his sap in buckets until twelve years ago, which made him one of the last of the old-time producers. He swore he'd never switch to the vacuum tubing, but he saw the light in 1990.

"The buckets were just too much work," he says. Besides, driving a tractor through the bush wasn't good for the trees. With the tubes, Glenn does everything on foot, which is a lot easier on the tree roots and on Glenn too. If it wasn't for the thimbleberries.

"My hands are completely scratched, and I have scratches on my nose and chin," he says.

Glenn started tapping last weekend. Every time he drills into a tree to insert a spout, Glenn gets to do something not many people can do. He gets to peer backwards through time. With every hole he drills, he can see the growth rings in the creamy sap wood, back through 2000 and 1999, back into 1998. He says from what he can see, the trees that didn't have their crowns mowed off by the ice storm, which went through his bush like a lawn mower, seem to have been doing well over the past four years. The light that is encouraging the thimbleberries is also shining on the surviving trees.

"The bush," says Glenn, "is slowly recovering."

What Glenn, and everyone else who is making maple syrup, wants at this time of the year are warm days followed by cold nights. When that happens, the sap starts running up and down the sap wood and can be tapped on the way down.

The magic, the happy alchemy, transpires in Glenn's sugar shack. In a few short hours, he boils the cold, clear sap down until it turns into golden syrup. The tang of wood smoke from the fire box mixes with the sweet-smelling steam that bellows out of the evaporator. The cheery aroma gets into everything. A sugar shack, writes R.D. Lawrence in his book *Maple Syrup*, "is like a steam bath built inside the heart of a volcano."

Glenn says that after you've stayed up a few nights tending to the evaporator, you can almost imagine the trees breathing in and out as the sugar water runs up and down under the bark.

These days when all the smoke and fire you see on the television news comes from high-altitude bombs, and the sweet talk from generals in uniform and politicians with pointers, it is good to remember that there is a mud time close to home where the pool of decay underfoot is the wonderful smell of the earth waking up and the trees coming to life.

10 March 2002

EARLY APRIL 2009

The ice was off the pond this weekend, the water brackish, brown and windswept. A sign of spring for sure, but a chilly sort of sign. A harbinger, more than a hint of things to come.

On Sunday we went for a walk, and everyone and everything seemed to be softening. There was mud where the sun was hitting the road, and the dog got covered in burrs.

On Monday we got out of bed, cautiously, and peered through the blinds. The sky was blue and the sun bright, but the pond was frozen again. From the upstairs window it looked like the fragile ice that comes overnight on October puddles, as if it would have cracked explosively if we tried to cross it. But our galoshes are not high enough for the pond, and anyway, up close, we found it to be thicker than we expected, and blacker, more January than June, with lots of little brown leaves and other wintery moments caught in its iciness.

We tried to snap a piece of ice from the edge, and it came easily enough, bringing to mind those phony glass panes they break over cowboys' heads in the movies.

At lunch, on Tuesday, standing in the gravel lane, talking to the roofer who had come to repair the wreck of this winter, and listening to the crows, we heard the noon bell on the fire hall tower for the first time in months. Not because it hasn't been ringing, but because we haven't been out there to hear it.

Early April. One day summer, one day winter. A year of weather packed into a month. The month that shuffles its feet on your stoop, like a young man clutching a bouquet behind his back while the girl stands there thinking, *Get over yourself. Give me the flowers.* But she waits, like little you and me, the burr-covered dog wagging her tail by our sides, while the ice melts and freezes, melts and freezes. All of us waiting for the moment he leans toward her. All of us praying for the kiss.

6 April 2009

WORMS

Bass fishing opens this weekend, and that is good news for Roger Parson of New Hamburg, Ontario. Roger works part-time at the parts counter at Kitchener Tractor. Three days a week, however, Roger hits the road in his 1999 purple Dodge Caravan. He travels around servicing thirty second-hand vending machines that he has bought, modified and placed in gas stations and all-night variety stores from Lake Erie to Lake Simcoe.

"I never dreamed I would get into the vending business," says Roger, "but my wife got a tumour and can't work anymore, and we needed extra money, so I had to do something."

Something turned out to be the vending business. Of course, these days most of the things you could think of putting in a vending machine, and most of the places you could dream of putting them, have been scooped up by someone else. So Roger had to come up with something special. He chose worms.

He added nightcrawlers and spawn for good measure.

"I put them in used pop cans," says Roger. "I close them with a plastic lid."

He has worried that from time to time, in the dead of night, revellers have fed coins into his machines expecting a can of pop and received the shock of their lives when they opened their can of worms.

During fishing season Roger visits each of his vending machines once a week.

"I don't *have* to go that often," he says. "The worms will live for four weeks in there."

He says his best customers are kids.

"I can pretty well tell by sales the day school is out for the summer. My business doubles overnight when school gets out."

Roger says sometimes, if a kid comes up to buy when he is servicing a machine, he will give them a free can of worms.

"Like the other day," he says, "I was at a variety store in Alcona Beach and a little girl came up on her bike. She was maybe twelve years old, and she had her little brother with her, who was maybe eight. She told me she was taking him down to the dock to fish for perch. She seemed to know what she was doing. She said she hoped the water was warm enough for the fish to bite. I don't do it all the time, but I gave *her* a can."

It made me happy to learn that there were still kids getting on their bikes and taking their fishing rods down to the lake to fish for perch. I was under the impression that kids' lives were too organized these days for that sort of thing.

"Yeah," says Roger, "when we were younger we lived outdoors more than kids do today. And we were allowed to make more choices. Kids spend too much time indoors these days."

"With parents watching too closely," I added.

I asked him what it was about the girl on the bike that made him decide to give her the free worms.

"It was her friendliness," said Roger. "The way she smiled. And then when I gave her the worms, she said thank you and told me she would be back next week."

Then he shrugged. "Kids are my future," he said. "As long as kids keep fishing, I am going to be in business."

27 June 2004

SUMMER JOBS

T.S. Eliot opens his most renowned poem, "The Waste Land," with a line that has the enduring ring of truth. Eliot famously claims, "April is the cruellest month." I don't pretend to know what Eliot was thinking when he wrote that, but those words stuck in my college-aged brain when many other things I was exposed to back then didn't. April *is* the cruellest month when you are a university student. April brings a shower of tests and term papers, a gale of all-nighters and the desperation of cram sessions. It's the season of panic, and regret, and eye strain, and too much coffee. But April is done like dinner, and with God's good grace, the kingdom of summer will soon settle upon us. Goodbye Duo-Tangs, goodbye highlighters, goodbye backpacks full of binders and loose-leaf paper. All of them should be stuffed under the bed, into corners and cupboards, to languish until autumn, the real season of renewal, stirs the leaves and we have another chance at getting it right. Another chance, perhaps, at figuring out "The Waste Land."

Summer is coming. Before you know it, all there *will* be time for is the smell of the sun on your skin. Someone's cottage. Summer love. And, of course, a summer job.

I miss summer jobs. I like the idea of a lifetime that lasts three or four months. June. July. August. Beginning. Middle. End. A perfect span for a decent career—long enough to get good at the thing , even long enough to get tired of it, but not *sick* and tired of it.

Don't get me wrong. I'm not saying that summer jobs are easy, or satisfying, or even rewarding. Sometimes, a summer job is three months of struggle, another lesson from the long list of things you aren't cut out to do. Summer jobs can be exhausting, tedious and thankless.

But whether the work is satisfying or not, summer jobs open your eyes to the world around you. Summer jobs allow you to appreciate the hard work *others* do all year. Summer jobs give you an idea of what you want to do for the rest of your life. A few months to try on a new hat, a different existence, a fresh outlook. A summer job can be a leap into another world, and that has to foster understanding if nothing else.

And I have been wondering if the world might be a better place if we all hung up our backpacks in May or June, got up from our desks, walked away from the assembly lines of our lives and got ourselves a summer job.

I have, in summers past, been a construction worker, and a camp counsellor, and a busboy, but I have never been a waiter. I think I could be good at that, especially at one of those resorts that are only open for the summer and have staff quarters, and staff snacks, and, I am willing to bet, staff parties.

I think things might lighten up to everyone's benefit if all the lawyers and lecturers had to spend their summer flipping burgers while the mechanics got to try their hands at the law. Let the waiters play in the symphonies and the lady from the laundromat do ... whatever she wants. And let's all head to the lake on the weekends while there is still enough water to go around.

29 April 2007

SEPTEMBER

September is upon us. We knew it was coming. It happens every year around this time. We love September, yet every August we find ourselves hoping that the winds of summer will linger.

We are just about ready to start our vacations now, not end them. It wouldn't have to be a long one; things are more or less shipshape; just, say, a couple of weeks with nothing to do. We have long believed that what we need, more than a holiday in February, is an extra month slipped in between August and September. Maybe a three-week month, where all that is necessary is—nothing at all. Not exactly vacation, but not exactly work either—the secular equivalent of purgatory, where we are required only to hang around, to wait, and in the waiting achieve the holiness necessary to enter this month that is upon us now and that, like all holy things, will not wait for us.

6 September 2009

A LETTER TO A YOUNG FRIEND
HEADING BACK TO SCHOOL

Dear Sam,

September is here again, and with it, all the familiar September sounds: the shuffle of feet on stairs, the rattle of lockers opening and closing, the annual autumn bells. Echoes we all hear when September rolls in, of the schoolyards and the school days, both past and present, that are both present and not present.

I have been thinking about you amid these ringing bells and wondering what I could possibly give you to mark the moment—wondering if there was some small token I could wrap, some little thing that would ring bells for you, as you head off once again with your brave little bag of books.

I have been racking my brain for some perfect thing that would tell you I understand the complexity of this week. That I know that although the first day of school is a grand day, the grandest day of all in many ways, that even in its grandeur, in the grandeur of new shoes and shirts, new friends and old ones, new teachers and new classes, that it is a grand bag of tricks too, that it comes with exams, and papers, and other things that can go all too wrong.

People like to say that this is the week that marks the real new year. And why not? What could be more full of possibility than the first day of school? As full of potential as a toboggan at the top of a snowy hill, as a pencil hovering over a blank page, as the smile of that girl with the golden hair sitting in the front row.

But sometimes the snow melts and you're standing there with your toboggan, feeling a fool, the only one who didn't hear the weather forecast.

It is a complicated thing, this business of school. And it is in the complexity that the sorrow and sadness comes. The heavy burden of books that pile up, and the numbers that don't; the metaphors that lie on their backs with their little feet wiggling in the air.

Timetable and exams, projects and essays, all that stuff can build up and cause problems, and I was hoping this thing I would give you could acknowledge that stuff too.

My first idea was a dictionary. A blue, cloth-covered *Canadian Oxford*, with the title stamped in gold letters. If I gave you a dictionary, you would have all the words in the world. You could look them up and write them down in any way you wanted, and the wind would blow, and the bells would ring, and the lockers would slam, and teachers would be bewitched by your way with words, and that girl with the golden hair too.

I thought maybe a dictionary with gold letters on the cover would be just the thing.

Then I thought, maybe a new pair of shoes.

A brand new pair of sneakers, sneakers as heady as dandelion wine, a pair of Ray Bradbury's "Royal Crown Cream Sponge Para Litefoot tennis shoes," and when you put them on, you bounce like a kangaroo, and when you run, you run like a gazelle. Is it a pair of sneakers you need as you run to school?

Or what about lunch? What about lunch every day for a year? If I packed you a lunch of carrot sticks and raisins, and peanut butter sandwiches on soft white bread, with lots of jelly, the way you like it, the bread so fresh you dent it with your fingers just in the unwrapping. I thought if I wrapped your sandwich in wax paper and wrote little notes on the paper with a black felt pen, and slipped in some chocolate from time to time, that might do the trick.

I thought. And I thought. And I thought I could be your wordsmith, your shoemaker, or your chef.

But none of them seemed right. The shoes didn't fit. You forgot the lunch bag on the bus. And who needs more words anyway? There are words enough to go around.

And that is when I decided to give you this eraser. It is an original Pink Pearl—a little plug of pink rubber, with a point at both the ends, and a broad side too, the perfect size for mistakes, big or small. It will fit in your hand, whatever size your hands are, whether you are four or forty, five or fifty, and is something that will work today, and work tomorrow.

Best of all, it has, deep in its rubbery little heart, memories of a rubber tree in some thick forest. A gash in the bark. The *drip, drip* of sap. But more than that: the worried frown of a chemist too.

Because your eraser has been vulcanized, my friend. And even though I don't have the slightest idea what that means, I do have the deep conviction that if we all carried some small vulcanized thing with us at all times, we would have an easier go of it. And be less prone to explosive anger, road rage, yelling and the gnawing anxiety of our fears.

This is for you.

I wrapped it in this brown paper to give to you this morning, this first day of school. And I hope you will understand when you unwrap it that life's greatest treasures are the simple ones.

Take its measure, roll it between your fingers, put it in your pocket. It is all you will need to get through the year safely.

It will give itself up to correct your mistakes. Its sharp edges slowly rounding like a piece of sea glass, until all that's left of it are little pink smears on the pages of your life. What more could you ask of anything?

If I am right about this, with this eraser in your bag, you can risk it all. Exams will mean nothing to you.

They can roll out the big numbers, and all the arrhythmic poems, and you will knock them clean out of the park.

This year you get the pink eraser from the deep thick forest. I give it to you with my love, and these instructions: take it with you everywhere. You never know when you are going to make a mess, or where, just that you are bound to mess things up.

Don't mind mistakes.

Mistakes are how you learn.

You have an eraser.

Go ahead, make messes.

Then ... clean them up.

Try again.

6 September 2009

AUTUMN

We saw that snow fell on Saskatchewan this Thursday, and as we stared gloomily at the television reports and the video of cars spinning their wheels along the Trans-Canada Highway, someone remarked what a glorious October it has been here where we live. I, for one, will be sad to see this October go.

Every morning when we woke, I would get out of bed and head for the window, thinking our luck couldn't hold. Then I would open the curtains ever so cautiously and find myself staring at another blue sky. When I went down to fetch the morning paper, the air was always thin and cool and comfortable. Every day by noon it was nice enough to eat outside.

We followed the progress of the back garden with delight as it slowly turned into a thing we listened to rather than looked at, all tawny and brown and full of wind rustle. Just to be alive this October was enough.

Autumn is the most olfactory of seasons—the time of year I am most doglike. October is the month I follow my nose rather than my feet. The barnyard smells of woodsmoke and decomposing leaves give the neighbourhood an honest, country feel.

Yesterday the moon was a sliver of fingernail floating in the deep purple of the late afternoon. This October has given us autumn at its best, and in my books autumn at its best is as good as it gets.

On Tuesday there was a rusted pickup parked in front of my office filled with a bunch of garden tools and about a thousand ornamental cabbages. I rushed home to get my camera and anyone who was there to come and see.

"It is so beautiful," I said. "It fits the season perfectly. As if it had been art-directed rather than driven into the neighbourhood." But like October, by the time we got back, the truck was gone and I didn't get my picture.

John, the cat who lives two doors down, is by common agreement the strangest cat in the neighbourhood. John is a stray who showed up a few years ago and moved in with Gary and Pat, although he spends most of his time sitting, like a loaf of bread, in the middle of the road. So far he hasn't been hit. But John is the colour of marmalade and, more to the point, the colour of the leaves that now pretty well cover the street. John disappeared early in the week, and Pat and Gary spent an hour poking through the leaves in the gutter on both sides of the street believing that John had finally got his just dessert. He showed up the next morning. Tim, who lives next door, had let him into his house and gone out, forgetting John was there.

Soon we'll face the dark rains of November and then the snow that hit Saskatchewan, but until then we'll keep a weather eye for that truck full of cabbage and we'll savour the smell of smoke and the carpet of leaves that this morning covered everything in sight.

5 November 2000

PIANO TUNERS

The weather has turned. We have done all we can to get ready. The wood is stacked, the pump is drained, the window washers have come and gone, to wherever the window washers go when the weather turns (just try to get someone to wash your windows in December). The roofers have gone too, south no doubt, along with the butterflies, and the blackbirds, and the bluebirds, and all the other birds with brains enough to get out while the getting was good. The legs are off the picnic table, the boat is out of the lake, and when he knocked the other day, Pius, the letter carrier, was wearing mittens and a hat—as sure a sign of winter as any.

There is no turning back now. Those who are going are gone. There is nothing left for *us* to do but stand by the windows we should have washed and wait for the cold rain we know is heading our way, knowing in our hearts that when the rains are finished with us, the snow won't be far behind. Everyone says winter is going to be easier this year. Easier than what?

I know. I know. There are plenty of people who look forward to winter. Skiers, snowshoers, men with snowblowers, women with skates, someone somewhere who has a favourite winter coat they just can't wait to wear.

But there are plenty of others on the other end of the seesaw, clinging on for dear life. The gardeners and the golfers, the sailors and the street vendors, the little girl who lost her gloves at recess and walked all the way home with her knapsack, her bare hands so cold they ached.

And, of course, the piano tuners. No one longs for spring more than people who tune pianos.

Because of all the hardships that winter brings, to the plant you left outside that you should have brought in, to the pipes you should have drained, to poor old you; all that is nothing, a trifle, when compared to the sorrow this winter will bring to the pianos of the land.

Winter has murdered at least half the pianos of the country. And when you consider that a nine-foot concert grand, the piano of choice if you are planning a concert, can cost as much as $150,000, that is murder most foul.

If you want a piano to last more than a decade, you have to baby it. Like the piano at Place des Arts in Montreal, for example, which more than one pianist has told me is their favourite piano in the country. The piano at Place des Arts has its own humidity-controlled room where it rests, between shows, like a bottle of Burgundy's best.

I was talking to my friend John yesterday. John is a piano player. And I can tell you, like all piano players, from Tofino to Twillingate, John is suffering his annual bout of pre-winter despair.

It's winter's dryness that gets them. If you let a piano dry up, it can die in a decade. The soundboard has a natural arc. And if the soundboard dries, the arc flattens and a piano won't resonate. A note that could sustain for thirty seconds will disappear *just like that*. And don't get me going about dry pegboards.

There are corpses everywhere. And that is why pianists like Anton Kuerti arrive at concert halls with their bags of tools and dive into the bowels of these pianos in a desperate attempt to rebuild them before they play them.

But sadly, like summer and autumn, and most everything in this wintery world, once they are gone, you can't get them back.

We arrived at the Port Theatre in Nanaimo last month to find a note from piano tuner Jürgen Goering waiting for us on the piano bench.

Welcome back to Vancouver Island, read his note. *You know you are on the west coast when the piano technician comes in by rowboat to tune the piano for your show.*

Well, there will be little rowing between now and spring. Worse luck.

Get out the vitamin C. Get out the hot water bottle and get out the humidifier. And if you happen to know a piano tuner … get out your hankies.

23 November 2008

APPROACHING WINTER

I received a note earlier this week from Pond Inlet in Canada's northern Nunavut territory. My friend Ruby wrote to say that the sun has disappeared from the sky. *But my sun prisms,* wrote Ruby, *are still hanging in my window.* What Ruby didn't say was that where she lives, a land of twenty-four-hour darkness, the prisms in her window are hanging as an act of faith as much as anything.

Even here in the south you can sense the days shortening and feel the darkness of winter, which has already settled around Ruby's house, coughing its chilly way out of the arctic with little you and me in its sights.

The wind and rain battered Vancouver this week, and in the east the skies have been low and grey. I spent last weekend with my back to winter, my toque pulled low, raking the last of the leaves off the deck. Then I headed down to the lake and covered up the boat, something I should have done weeks ago, chastising myself as I fumbled with the blue plastic tarp.

It's getting dark. It's getting cold. It's been windy and wet. And we all know it's going to get darker, and colder, and windier before this winter is finished with us. To make matters worse, I just ate three Girl Guide cookies. And I'm sorry, but I don't even like Girl Guide cookies.

But, as you stand there on your corner with your umbrella blown inside out, and as I head down to my basement to see if the boots, and the mitts, and the scarves are anywhere to be found, there is something we should both remember. Up in Pond Inlet, in Ruby's house, that sun prism is still hanging in the window, and every once in a while, even in the dark arctic night, it catches the headlight from a snowmobile, or a water truck rumbling by, and each time it does, it gives off a brief flash of spring.

We spend our summers trying to get outside as much as we can. These are the nights it's good to be home.

There is still a month to go before the darkest day of the year, but with every passing day, we are not only moving closer to darkness, but to all of the festivals of light: Kwanza, Hanukkah, Diwali, Christmas. And to your birthday, for that matter, and to the happy day when the sun rises just that little bit earlier, lingers a little longer.

19 November 2006

HIBERNATION

I like winter, so I am always excited to see it come. I like to ski and to skate, and on a good night, I even like to shovel snow. There is a lot to enjoy in winter—fires and hot chocolate to name a few others—but every winter, by this time, no matter how happy I was at the beginning, I begin to wonder if maybe the fires and the hot chocolate are the best part of it, if the best part of being cold is getting warm.

There have been Marches in my life when I have wondered if I am solar-powered. By the beginning of every March, I always feel like I need more sun than I have been getting. And although I enjoy winter, I would be lying if I didn't tell you there have been Februarys when I have wondered if I wouldn't have been happier as a bear, so I could hibernate. Now there is a bit of genetic modification that someone should take a close look at. Do we really *need* to clone sheep?

If a geneticist truly wanted to make a contribution, she should take a look at hibernation. If you were watching late-night television, and someone came on and offered a hibernating gene for three easy payments of—well, I am betting she could just about name her price—I for one would be reaching for my chequebook. Imagine a day in November, when it has been raining since dawn. It is now four-thirty in the afternoon, and getting dark, and you are standing in the kitchen looking at a wet dog, when someone comes on the television and says, *Would you like to go to bed for three months?* I'm reaching for my pyjamas, calling the kids into the bedroom and telling them this: *I am going to slow my heart down to about a beat a minute, and there is nothing in the world you are going to be able to do to stir me. I am not going to wake up until April, and when I do, I am going to be cranky, and hungry, so you better be careful.*

I don't care what the kids do. The kids can stay up if they want. That's what they always want to do anyway. They can do science experiments with me as far as I care. They can stick my hand in a bucket of warm water to see what happens; makes no matter, I am just going to keep on snoring.

How much would I pay for that gene? I don't know, but I know I'd be buying.

I think my plan would be to get up just in time for the playoffs, which is pretty much how it works now anyway.

3 March 2002

SALT OF THE EARTH

There seems to be more salt on the streets this winter than there used to be. Or at least on the sidewalks. Or at least on the sidewalks of my neighbourhood. My evidence for this observation is purely anecdotal and would not impress a scientist. I rest my claim not on the back of rigorous observation but on the back of my dog. Or, rather, her paws. Barely a night passes when I am out with the dog that she doesn't begin to limp, and we don't have to stop. We have worked out a routine that we both understand. She holds up the leg that hurts, I take off my glove and pick out the salt crystal that is causing her distress.

Some nights, when it is too cold for a sensible man to be squatting on the sidewalk cleaning his dog's feet with his bare hands, I have wondered about buying her a set of the little dog boots you see small dogs wearing from time to time in the city, but I can't bring myself to do that. We may live in the city, and I may enjoy my city life, but I have worked on a farm, and it is hard for me to do anything that might bring a smirk to the face of a farmer.

Here in the city where I live, homeowners are responsible for shovelling the public sidewalk in front of their houses. A growing number of my neighbours, it seems, are turning to salt, rather than shovels, to fulfill their civic duty.

You can hardly blame them. That's the tactic the city has chosen to keep the roads clear. Salt has become the first, rather than the last, line of defence in the war against snow.

Toronto is so committed to salt that the city is ringed with seven salt camps. These camps are set up like army bivouacs and include trailers that are staffed around the clock, complete with cots and kitchens—camps of truck drivers paid to stand by so the moment snow begins to fall, they can run for their salt trucks. City officials expect them to be on the road within *five* minutes of the first snowflakes.

The same officials say they have tested and rejected other alternatives. Calcium magnesium acetate is too expensive. Sand, I am told, is not without its own environmental problems. They even tried a liquid called MAGIC, a by-product of the beer industry that they sprayed on the streets, with mixed results, sadly.

Toronto has 118 salt trucks in service this winter, and those trucks will dump in the neighbourhood of 125,000 tons of salt on city streets. My neighbours will add to that.

It is a practice the ancients would find beyond belief. Homer called salt *divine.* Plato named it a substance *dear to the gods.*

But Homer and Plato lived in warmer climes and at a time when salt was so highly prized, and so difficult to obtain, that religious significance was attached to it. A meal where salt was served was sacred. It created connections and the Arabic phrase, *There is salt between us.*

The Greeks, the Romans and the ancient Jews all used salt in sacred ways. While the Germans fought wars over saline streams.

Some academics believe the oldest roads were the salt roads that the clattering salt caravans followed through the Sahara and the deserts of Libya. One of the oldest roads in Italy is the Via Salaria.

So it seems that in some way salt has always been linked to roadways, although in the ancient days the roads were there for the salt, rather than the other way around.

Today, Canada is the fourth largest producer of salt in the world. From salt mines in Windsor and Goderich, Ontario, from Pugwash, Nova Scotia, and from the Magdalen Islands, Canada produces more salt than it needs—enough surplus to export tons to the United States.

This salt, the salt we send abroad and the salt we see on the streets, the salt we pass around our tables, the salt that I pick out of my dog's paws, all comes from ancient deposits, remnants of long-forgotten oceans.

And now, I read, that if the mines ever ran out, there is enough salt suspended in the world's oceans to make five full-sized relief models of Europe.

So we don't feel profligate when, in the darkness of December, we greet snow by scattering salt at our feet. And, as we do, we may well be reaching back to some ancient memory, and saying, in our own way, that these streets where we live are holy streets, worthy of keeping clear; and the white florets of salt that marble them in the cold winter mornings are there to remind us that we are *the salt of the earth;* and the trucks criss-crossing the city in the winter nights are prayer trucks, reminding us in the dark of the winter, when the snow piles around us, that we have nothing to fear, that we are not alone, that we are here for each other, for there is *salt between us.*

5 February 2000

FEBRUARY

February is the oddest of the months and not my favourite. And here, stuck in the middle of it, I am looking forward to the day when I can watch February fade into the rear-view mirror of the year.

I know February does have Valentine's Day, which recommends it to some—to the glad spenders, and the hawkers of roses, and all the fancy dancers who know the right things to say to a girl or to a boy when they catch their eye—but I'm with Carl Sandburg on this: Valentine's Day has taught me more about the taste of cabbage than the mystery of roses.

It *is* the month my mother was born, but apart from that, and the odd flutter from Sandburg's little white bird of love, February has added up to just too much winter. The Fathers of Confederation, or the trickster Raven, or whoever it was who designed the month must have agreed. They did their best to whittle away at it, doling out twenty-eight meagre days in most years, grudgingly handing out a twenty-ninth from time to time. Why they didn't just do away with the whole month while they were at it, and add the twenty-eight days to say, June, when love is *really* in the air, or September, a month I have always thought should be longer, is beyond me.

But they didn't, and we are stuck with it, and this year, being one of the years when February has twenty-nine days instead of twenty-eight, we are stuck with it more than ever.

It is a curious construction, this notion that a month can accordion in and out every four years—I don't know how they got that past the board of regents. You are commissioned to codify the year, to design a system that makes the year solid and reliable, and you do that eleven out of twelve months, but then it's as if you shrug and say, "What the heck? I'm hungry. I'm going home." You leave February to some maniac from the basement who has radical theories about child-rearing, and what you should eat for breakfast, and has been just waiting for a chance like this. He gets February in a thumb grip, and this is what we are left with: a month that can't keep track of itself. A month that loses days willy-nilly. Days fluttering out the backpack of the month and vanishing into thin air like those school notices your kids never bring home.

It's Leap Year, which any sensible person might conclude means we leap ahead, skip out of February a day early in our headlong lunge to spring, but this *being* February—a month, upon reflection, I am beginning to think of as more perverse than odd—it means our leap is a leap to nowhere, a leap to where we started, stuck in this month, sometimes a day short, sometimes with more days on our hands than we want. Perhaps the best idea this Leap Year is to embrace that other February holiday—Groundhog Day. I'm pretty sure I saw my shadow. I'm going back to bed. Wake me in March.

24 February 2008

SNOWMAN

My favourite moment of the winter past was the afternoon we stumbled upon the snowman on Howland Avenue. It was the biggest snowman I have ever seen. It had a base bigger than a Volkswagen and took up most of the front lawn where it stood.

Intrigued, I knocked on the front door and introduced myself to the man who answered. His name was John Keefer. John told me he had built his snowman on a Friday night in February. He says he was just "inspired by the moment." The air was warm that night, he said, or as warm as it had been all winter, and the snow on his front lawn was piled as high as he'd ever seen it. And it was perfect packing snow. John started building his snowman before dinner. He went out after he finished eating to finish the job.

John said he worked in the dark, knowing that his two-year-old daughter, Elsie, would wake up Saturday morning to a snowman as big as a buffalo.

When he finished, John rooted through his recycling box and found a face for his snowman. He used a bright green cap from a detergent bottle as a nose and a yellow plastic peanut butter lid for the mouth. He fashioned red eyes with lids from two pickle jars.

He said the temperature dropped that night and turned the snow as hard and strong as cement, making his snowman a fixture in the neighbourhood. All through February, local kids came to play with it, adults brought their friends, teenagers dropped by just to hang out.

After a few days, a handful of pennies appeared in the trench that surrounded the snowman. By the end of the first week there was nearly a dollar of change in the trench.

John says he isn't sure what the money was about. I like to think each penny came with a wish, maybe for an early spring, or for a warm summer.

I never know what to do with my pennies. But scattering them around a snowman and wishing for warm weather does not seem like such a foolish thing to do in the middle of February—seems like a particularly Canadian thing to, so this summer we'll be saving as many as we can, and we will keep them for the dark days of *next* winter when we are really going need a wish or two.

22 March 2004

NOTES FROM THE NEIGHBOURHOOD

BOY, BIKE, CHAIR

I was on my way to the grocery store when I spotted him. A boy, about eleven years old I guessed, riding his bike up the middle of the street. He was riding awkwardly, weaving from side to side, as he was holding on to the handlebars with one hand and to an office chair with the other. The chair, which was black and was also on wheels, had clearly seen better days.

"That looks like hard work," I said.

"Yup," said the boy, not unhappy someone had noticed.

Then he stopped pedalling and stood, astride his bike, pleased, it occurred to me, to have an excuse to rest for the moment. Resting is not something eleven-year-old boys do intuitively. I was happy to provide the excuse.

"You taking that home?" I asked.

The boy nodded.

"Nice day for it," I said.

I tried to keep my questions non-threatening. I was, after all, a stranger. I assumed he had been warned about talking to people like me.

"My name's Stuart," I said

"My name's Matt," he said.

Then he said, "When I get home I am going to tie a rope to this chair and pull it behind my bike, and my friend is going to ride in it. Then we are going to switch."

He smiled proudly.

I smiled back, imagining all sorts of horrible things: the chair careening around in traffic, the rope breaking, cuts, bruises, broken bones.

I almost said, "Be careful." I restrained the impulse. He presumably had parents to tell him that. *And* to warn him about talking to people like me.

"Sounds great," I said. Then because I couldn't think of anything else to say, I shrugged, and said, "I gotta go."

"Me too," he said.

I stood there for a moment and watched him pedal up the street, part of me wishing he had said those magic words of boyhood. *Wanna come?* Remembering with great fondness, those days when a broken chair, a piece of rope and a bicycle were all you needed to make the world perfect.

1 October 2006

TORONTO

The celebrated Canadian geographer Cole Harris once described the *inhabited* part of Canada as an island archipelago spread over four thousand east-west miles.

Professor Harris's archipelago spreads farther if you factor in all the islands of the great north, and is as thoughtful and encompassing a description of Canada as any, and better than most. It accommodates both the *distances* and *differences* that make Canada so surprisingly watertight. And, as an analogy, it holds up well when measured against the rocky shores of our many cultures, against the still waters of our tolerance, and against all the other tidal surges that both pull us apart and push us back together, endlessly and relentlessly.

I like how it makes me think about Canada, but also, I should say, I like how it allows me to think about myself. Because if we *are* a chain of islands, stretched along the border, well, that makes me the island-hopper. And, I have to say, I like the sound of that.

I spend a good part of my life, these days, hopping around the country. But when I am not—hopping, that is—Toronto is the place I return to. Toronto is my home, and when I come home, I always feel a little like I am *leaving* the islands and returning to the mainland—which is, I suppose, how you should feel about coming home, wherever your home is, whether it be a city home, a country home, in a big town or small one, or even on an island. Home should feel like solid ground.

This city hasn't always been my home. I was born and raised on the island of Montreal. I know Montreal the way you know the town of your boyhood. I know it intuitively.

Toronto is a city I had to learn.

I came, some thirty years ago, because CBC Radio asked me to. I came for my work. I didn't give my coming, or, more importantly, my leaving, a moment's thought. I departed Montreal on the waves of my youthful enthusiasm. Although, like so many others who leave their hometowns, I left believing it would only be a year or two before I returned.

But those years add up, and now, all these years later, I find that I have lived in Toronto longer than I lived in the city where I was born.

Toronto is my home now. And whether I admit it or not, it is my home by choice.

When I travel across the country and talk turns to hometowns, people often look at me with compassion when they learn where I live. *Oh, I wouldn't want to live there,* they say. Often they don't say it quite that directly, but I can see it in their eyes and hear it in the things they choose to tell me about *their* hometowns.

I wouldn't want to live in a place where you don't know your neighbours. Where people are in such a hurry. Where the driving is so impossible. I counted sixteen lanes on that highway near the airport.

Well, yes. It is heavy lifting living in a big city. No doubt about that. But not in the way those who don't live in one might think.

This city asks a lot of those of us who live here. But there is much to love too.

Like all of the other islands in the Canadian archipelago, Toronto has a romance with water. It is built on the shore of a lake and organized around the banks of two rivers—the Don and the Humber still wander pleasantly through the city, and if you wander along their banks or through any of the many ravines that bisect the city, you can run into deer, coyote, rabbits, fox and skunk right in the heart of town.

More than the gentle slope of the hills leading down from the old lakeshore to the shore of the lake; more than the streets, or the streetcars, or the swoop of the Don Valley Parkway at night, all soft and yellow and winding; more than the gracious parks or the grinding parking lots; more than the corner stores, or the late-night stores; more than the stock market, or the St. Lawrence Market, or the meat markets; more than the low-rises or the high-rises, the theatres on King, and the galleries on Queen; more than the one, two, three, *four!* newspapers; more than the Blue Jays or the Maple Leafs, the Stanley Cup or the World Series; more than the restaurants and the cafés; more than these things, or any number of other things any of us could name, Toronto is a conversation.

It is a conversation that began before any of us were born. Back when the Don River ran clean and clear. A conversation that began before us, and continues with and without us every hour of the day.

And this is what this city asks of us. This is the heavy lifting. It asks that we participate in the conversation. More than ask, it demands that of us. And it is through this great civic conversation that the city lives.

Those of us concerned with the natural world talk about the parks and the rivers and the quiet places: the street corners and the canopy of trees; others of us, taken up by the world of commerce, concern ourselves with buildings and building, and the getting and the spending of time and money.

And no matter, because whichever one I am, what my neighbours want to know is where do I stand on the idea of an island airport? An expanded subway? Swimming pools in the schools? Green bins? And blue bins?

And when I am sure of my opinion, when I have thought about it, and talked about it, when I have figured it all out, and I am standing at the finish line, all huffing and puffing and proud, that's when the city tells me to tie up my shoes and keep running: I am not close to the finish line.

Because once I know where I stand on these and any number of other things, this city requires something more of me. It requires me to accommodate where others stand.

Where they stand on this, and on that, and also on music played late at night, and when sidewalks should be shovelled, and where and how one parks one's car.

This is what the city asks of us. It asks us to participate in the grand conversation and then, when we do, to be mindful of the others who are talking too—to accommodate them and their different ways and their voices of many languages.

This may be an urban jungle, but the ecology here is more swamp than forest. It is rich, and fetid, and varied, and different, and you have to look a little harder to see the beauty here, away from the mountains and the forests and the pristine lakes. But if you can catch the light just right, the beauty can be just as dazzling.

I don't think there is a nicer thing in the world than a morning walk in a Toronto neighbourhood. Any neighbourhood will do—the city is full of them. A walk in Toronto is especially lovely if it is late in the summer, and there are trees arcing over the sidewalk, and the odd corner store, and boxes of grapes, and circles of unshaven Italian men in their dress pants and vests getting ready to make wine.

I had to leave town soon after I moved into the house where I live today. I moved in, stayed for a couple of weeks, and then I had to go away. I had been gone maybe a week when I received a phone call from one of my new neighbours.

"You left the window of your car open," she said. "It is going to rain. Can I get a key and close it?"

There was no way she could do that.

"The car will just have to get wet," I said. "It will be okay. Things that get wet, dry."

When I got home, I found my car covered with a tarpaulin. But not by the neighbour who had called, by another one, who had also taken stock of my predicament.

The thing is, I *do* know my neighbours. The thing is, when it comes down to it, we all live in small towns. Mine happens to be in the heart of a big city. I follow my own footsteps back and forth to Peter's little butcher shop, to Potts's grocery store, over to Herman's hardware, and Sal's, where I get produce, to the place I go to get my hair cut, and the coffee shop up the street.

They know me in these places. And I know them.

This is my home. And, yes, sometimes living here is hard work, but maybe the best thing about the city is that it asks so much of me, because the thing it asks is for me to be my best self. To be a citizen.

We are blessed to be here. To have so much when so many have so little. To live, by God's grace, in a wonderful country. And by great good luck, to be part of the conversation that is Toronto.

28 February 2010

THE PARKING SPOT

I had driven my car to Kensington Market, and I was looking for a place to park on the street, which made me either an optimist or a fool—more the fool, I knew, because I was also in a hurry.

Kensington Market, in the heart of Toronto's Chinatown, is not a place in which you can be in a hurry, especially in a car. The streets are narrow, and the stores are small and crowded. People and piles of garbage spill off the sidewalk. The driving is difficult. The parking, impossible. I should have known better.

But there I was, inching along in my foolish optimism. And then, miracles of miracles, I spotted a parking space just a car's length in front of me.

It was immediately clear, however, that I wasn't going to get the spot. There was a car inching along ahead of me. The driver had seen the same thing I had. He was now slowing, stopping, twisting in his seat, preparing to back in.

This is what happened next.

The parking spot turned out to be only *hypothetically* free. A group of people (a family, it seemed to me) was standing in the spot, attempting, I could only guess, to reserve it for someone who was, I assume, somewhere in the line of cars behind me. A woman, who looked like the mother of this family, was standing in the spot, waving at the guy ahead of me. She was telling him *not* to back into the spot. She was indicating the spot was already hers.

The guy in the car clearly didn't want to listen to her. He sat there, half in, half out of the spot, and I realized we had a situation on our hands.

Nobody moved for a couple of minutes. Not the mother, not the man, and not me. I couldn't leave until this was resolved. The woman was blocking the parking spot. The man was blocking the street.

So I sat there trying to work out whose side I was on, until the man in the car got impatient and began to back up right into the woman. Or *almost* into the woman. She gave way. The man scooped the spot. The road ahead of me was clear. I could proceed.

Suddenly it seemed important for me to say something before I left. I slowed down and I glared at the man in the car, and then I gestured at him, not obscenely, but in a way that communicated to him that I disapproved of what he had just done. Then I drove away.

On reflection, it occurred to me that in some ways the man in the car had done the right thing. Given the dynamics of the crowded market, that woman shouldn't have been trying to hold on to the parking spot. It wasn't good manners. But given that she *was,* given her *bad* manners, the man in the car hadn't helped the greater good by picking a fight.

Even if right is on your side, when someone yells at you, it is not often helpful to yell back—especially if you're using two tons of steel to do your yelling.

I'm not sure about my part in all this. I'm not sure why I felt the need to add my two cents, and I know by doing so I wasn't being helpful.

"You were the witness," said a friend of mine when I told him what had transpired.

"It's important," said my friend, "that when we are a witness, that we bear witness."

Maybe.

Or maybe it's important that we keep our counsel and remember that when people are rude or unpleasant, they are rude and unpleasant for a reason. They are teachers sent, of course, to teach us, over and over again, the big lessons of patience and forgiveness.

19 March 2006

GARBAGE

I was at my desk, working at something or other and totally absorbed by it, when a part of me that I wasn't paying attention to noticed it was smelling something peculiar.

This wasn't a pleasant smell. It was a solvent of some sort. The closest thing I could compare it to had I been conscious of it would be model airplane glue. But I couldn't describe it because I was too preoccupied to notice this unpleasant smell, except, as I say, unconsciously. It tugged at my consciousness for the better part of an hour, until slowly I became aware not only that the smell was there, but that it was making me feel nauseous and then, all of a sudden, headachy, which is when it burst onto centre stage like an actor in a hurry. I stopped writing and went downstairs to ask Louise, who comes in three mornings a week and was working away herself.

"Louise," I said, "Do you …"

"… smell something funny?" she said, finishing my sentence for me.

At that moment, this peculiar smell became the only thing I was preoccupied with, and I began doing the useful sort of things a man does when these things happen. I began to sniff my way around the house. Pretty soon I had worked out that the solvent smell was stronger in the basement than anywhere else.

Now this is a new basement we are talking about. Well, actually, it is an old basement. But it was new to me. I had, only the week before, moved into this house, a modest Victorian in a row of Victorians, built, I am told, in 1899, and now smelling like there was a classroom of kids hidden away somewhere building model planes. Or worse. And this was giving me some concern, not to mention a headache. And doubts about my purchase.

Not knowing what to do next, I went next door and knocked on my neighbour's door. We hadn't met.

"I am your new neighbour," I said. "And I was wondering if ..."

"I smell something funny?" she said, finishing my sentence for me.

Exactly, I nodded.

"It seems," she said, "to be stronger in my basement."

I decided to phone the fire department.

"It is not actually an emergency," I explained. "I would rather you didn't turn on the sirens."

I was hoping for a couple of discreet guys with a meter of some description. Of course I got sirens vectoring in on my house from both the north and south. Three fire trucks, an ambulance and the fire chief in a red van. And a crowd of neighbours.

That was when I started wishing I had checked my basement a little more carefully—for that forgotten tube of model glue that had, no doubt, burst in the move.

That's what I was thinking, in any case, as I stood on the

sidewalk and watched the firefighters tramping into my basement. So I was delighted when other neighbours began to report the same smell.

"They have it in the house across the street," said a man in a plaid shirt to the fire chief.

Pretty soon the firefighters were knocking on doors up and down the street, which meant they were treating my call seriously; and I don't mind saying that was a relief.

After about half an hour, a consensus was beginning to emerge. The consensus was that a gas station about a block away had dumped solvent into the sewer system, and the smell was backing up through our drainpipes.

The guy across the street had apparently watched people at the garage do just this on numerous occasions. Mostly at night. He had, apparently, reported them before.

"I can't believe it," I said. "Who would do that sort of thing?"

"It happens," said the assistant fire chief, whose name was Liam and who used to be a cop in Galway.

"There are," he said, "legal proceedings outstanding against these guys."

I know it happens. I know it is expensive, and difficult, and often disruptive to follow environmental codes. And I know there are people, when faced with a forty-five-gallon drum of solvent, who take the easy way out; but I couldn't believe this was happening right under my nose.

"I can't believe it," I said to the firefighter. And to a couple of others standing around.

What I didn't tell them, however, is what I had done myself, earlier in the week.

Like I said, I had just moved into the neighbourhood, and earlier in the week, as I unpacked, I was faced with a mountain of green garbage bags that I had filled with the newsprint that the movers had used to wrap my china and CDs and lamps and ... everything else that I owned that was remotely fragile.

So garbage day is Friday in my new neighbourhood. Or every second Friday actually: it is garbage one Friday and recycling the next. It was garbage day the first Friday after I moved in. And there I was, faced with a mountain of garbage bags filled with recyclable paper. By rights I should have held on to those bags for a week. But I didn't have a place to store them for a week. I could have piled them on my deck, I guess, but I was taken up by the idea that I should settle into my new house as quickly as possible. And settling in meant getting rid of those garbage bags full of paper. Instead of letting them sit on the deck for a week, I hauled them out to the curb and let the garbage collectors take them away.

And what I want to know is this: *what is the difference between me and those hoodlums in that garage?*

We both had something that we wanted to get rid of. And we both turned to the easiest and least inconvenient solution. We both turned to the solution at hand.

And I know sending my bags of newsprint to the landfill instead of to the recycling plant is not the end of the world and is, on whatever scale you want to measure it, small potatoes compared to dumping a forty-five-gallon drum of solvent into the city's sewer system.

But I didn't have a forty-five-gallon drum of chemicals at

hand. I just had the bags of newsprint. And it seems to me in the grand scheme of things, I didn't do any better than they did at all. And my question is, if I *did* have the chemicals, could I trust myself to do better?

19 February 2006

HAIRCUTS
BY CHILDREN

I was walking my bike down by the lake when I spotted my friend Ian walking toward me.

"Hey," I said after we had said hello, "what the heck is up with your hair?"

Ian, who has a beard and tends to sit on the shaggy end of the scale, looked a bit, how do I describe this? He had a new 'do, which was dramatically short on the sides, yet, well, it didn't look like it had been touched on top. It made him look ...

"Like Lyle Lovett?" asked Ian hopefully.

"More like a mushroom," I suggested.

"That's what *I* thought," said Ian morosely.

Then he told me he had just had it cut at an art installation. By an eleven-year-old.

The event was called *Haircuts by Children*.

The haircuts, explained Ian, were free. The point of the exercise was to make adults rethink their perceptions of kids.

"And have you rethought yours?" I asked.

"In a roundabout sort of way," said Ian, running his hands through his hair, or what was left of it.

Then he explained something that had transpired while he

was sitting in the barber chair and eleven-year-old Anthony circled him with clippers and scissors.

"The most interesting thing happened in the chair beside me," said Ian.

There were, he explained, four barber chairs in the room. At the one beside him, an eleven-year-old girl was standing on her tiptoes so she could work on an elderly woman with wavy grey hair.

"The two of them were chatting back and forth, just like in a real salon," said Ian. "It was very charming. And then, in the middle of this, the old lady turned to the girl and apologized.

"'I am sorry,'" she said, "'that my hair is so greasy and tangled. I didn't have time to wash it this morning.'"

That is the sort of thing you probably hear muttered every day in salons across the country.

"But that's not the point," said Ian, who was starting to perk up.

"The point," he continued, "is what the little girl said in return. She said, 'Yeah, your hair is greasier and more tangled than any hair I have ever seen.'"

The lady, apparently, smiled. And after a slight pause, the two of them were chatting as easily as before.

Ian was really excited now.

"Imagine if everyone was that honest," he said.

"Imagine if you were trying on a pair of jeans, and you asked the salesperson how they made you look, and she said, 'Actually, not very good. They make you look fat.'

"Or imagine if you called a lawyer, and he told you, 'Sure, I'd be happy to do that, but it will cost you seven hundred dollars, and you'll be totally confused when I'm finished.'"

As we move through this life, we hear many variations of the truth. We answer each other, more often than not, with attempts to please or influence, or at least not offend, instead of informing each other with sincerity.

"Exactly," said Ian. "We are all too worried of offending. Imagine how great it would be if everyone was as honest as that little girl. All the time."

Ian had obviously been inspired.

"It has really got me thinking," he said.

We stood there for a while on the sidewalk and laughed about his haircut.

"I'm going to get it fixed this afternoon," he said. "I'm going to the barber. It'll be fine."

"What did you tell the kid?" I wondered.

"Oh," said Ian, smiling, "I told him it was the best haircut I ever had."

"What?" I said.

"It's the truth," said Ian. "It was."

23 July 2006

THE WORLD CUP

It has been a week now and World Cup celebrations are just about over in Toronto. All that's left this morning is the odd flag flapping from the window of the odd car, a windy reminder that June 2002 was one of the most joyfully rambunctious months that has ever blown through this old city.

The games were a tutorial for students of urban geology. They learned, if they didn't already know, that the tectonics of the city's ethnic alliances run along east-west lines. Italians went to gnash their teeth in the cafés and bistros along either St. Clair Avenue or College Street. Shoehorned between them, along Bloor Street, deposited there during a different geological epoch, the astounded Koreans ran amok in their red T-shirts, with their whistles and chants. The Portuguese had Dundas to themselves until Portugal was eliminated, and then they tucked their pennants away, picked up the lighthearted green-and-blue Brazilian flag and moved up to College, bumping up on the eastern edge of all those dispirited Italians.

What a month it was.

If you lived in any of these neighbourhoods, you had two

options. You could pull your drapes over your windows and your pillow over your head and try to sleep. That is to say that you could watch the games through your squinted and sleep-deprived eyes and cheer desperately for the team that would celebrate its victory farthest from *your* house, or you could let it rip. You could, if you lived near Bloor and Christie, do just as the Korean T-shirt of favour urged: you could *Be the Reds.* For ten bucks you could *buy* one of those Red Devil T-shirts and plunge right into this great and unexpected shift in the city's social crust.

That's what the cops eventually did. At first they showed up at the street parties and stood around on the corners in little blue clusters while whistle-blowing mobs brought traffic to a standstill. Their instincts told them they should keep the streets open, but, thankfully, someone along the chain of command figured out that clearing the streets would be a mistake, intuited that something more important than the flow of traffic was moving through the city.

By the quarter-finals, even the police understood that these were fun-loving crowds, and in a remarkable act of civic trust and good spirit, the police stopped showing up. They handed the streets over to the whistle-blowers, and the taxi drivers and delivery people did what the rest of us did, the only sensible thing anyone could do—whenever they were gridlocked by joy, they started honking their horns and hanging out their windows and high-fiving the kids with the flags.

It was, unquestionably, the Koreans who led the way. It was the Koreans who really got the city going. When the Turks wanted to celebrate their victories, they found themselves without a neighbourhood of their own. They solved that problem by gathering in joyful Koreatown, where they were welcomed with open arms. For most of June, the Turks and Koreans celebrated their victories together.

This sense of communal joy, which was as much a celebration of ethnic viability and community as it was a celebration of any particular game, a great bursting of national and neighbourhood pride, was captured one last time at the corner of Ossington and College last Saturday morning, an hour after Brazil defeated Germany in the final match.

Eric Timm, a forty-six-year-old schoolteacher of German descent, watched that last game in an Italian café. All month Timm had been driving around Toronto on his motorcycle—flying a giant German flag on an eight-foot-tall flagpole. When Saturday's game was over, Timm wanted to give his flag one last whirl. At first he didn't know where to go, and then he felt a responsibility well up in him. The German team he had been cheering for, that had come so far in the tournament, had to be represented at the victory celebrations. And Timm knew it had fallen to him to make that happen.

Timm climbed onto his yellow 1974 Honda 750 and headed for the heart of the Brazilian street party. He only intended to drive by, but when he got there and saw he was the only German around, he was seized by the need to make a statement. He parked his bike at the corner of Ossington and College, at the epicentre of the celebrations, and he climbed up onto his seat. And he stood there like a sentry for three hours.

He cut an imposing figure. He was wearing an Indonesian shirt knotted under his navel, black jeans, motorcycle boots and Ray-Bans. He hadn't shaved for five days.

"I guess I was a bit of an item," he said.

You could see him from a quarter-mile away, the black, red and gold flag of Germany sticking twelve feet up in the air beside him.

"I didn't go without trepidation," said Timm. "It was a bit of an experiment. I wanted to know how I would be received. I wanted to know if this really was what it seemed to be."

The answer, as it was *all* month, was a resounding Yes.

"Brazilians high-fived me and bought me drinks," he said. "Brazilians came over to me to talk about the game. Brazilians asked me to pose for pictures with their wives. They commiserated with me. And they consoled me. They told me the German team was still young. They told me Germany would have another crack in four years."

That night the moon hung over Toronto like a big white soccer ball. On Monday one of the city's newspapers said June was a glorious celebration of multiculturalism. They were almost right. But it wasn't a *celebration* of multiculturalism. It was the real thing. It *was* multiculturalism. There has been a lot of talk over the last twenty years about the richness of Toronto's diverse communities. From time to time those of us lucky enough to live here get to see that first-hand.

7 July 2002

THE FRONT LAWN

The idea of the suburbs in the United States, I have read, can be traced to the journalist and father of American landscape architecture, Frederick Law Olmsted. Olmsted, who designed Central Park among many others, became suspicious of downtown neighbourhoods, like mine, and went in search of what he called "a holy green environment," neighbourhoods that he believed would be better for the health of the family. Olmsted's idea was to create housing developments with the look of a park—and thus the front lawn was born, and the notion that families who believed in the greater good would "keep up their lawn."

At the heart of Olmsted's philosophy was his belief that "landscape has an effect on the unconscious" and his assumption that the best effect is achieved by "a gently rolling landscape of green."

It was an assumption that made so much intuitive good sense that no one thought to question it. Or no one where I grew up, or lived, ever questioned it. So pretty soon everyone had a front lawn. And pretty soon the competitive spirit raised its head, and the quest for the perfect lawn became so obsessive that grass was so vigorously weed-whacked, sprayed and rolled that it lost its connection with holiness, and lawns began to look worryingly more like living room rugs than any holy thing.

I can mark exactly where and when the rebellion began in my neighbourhood. The Dunker family down the street—Europeans—plowed up their front yard and let it lie fallow for a season. They wanted to see what would come if they let nature take its course. What came was goldenrod, of course, and Queen Anne's lace, blue chicory, buttercup, dandelions, and bunches of other wild and native plants, until eventually what came were the weed police. The weed police told the Dunkers they couldn't do what they were doing. They had to have a front lawn.

That was ten years ago.

One night this week, I realized that the Dunkers were, like most rebels, just slightly ahead of their time. The seller of lightning rods, as Ray Bradbury wrote, arrives just before the storm. Over the last decade there has been a slow but steady shift in the front yards that I walk by. Flowerbeds have been creeping over their borders, overflowing their boundaries and spilling out over the grass. There are no longer lawns in front of a good 50 percent of the houses I pass—all through my neighbourhood the front lawn has been shrinking to the point of disappearing.

One of my favourite yards is completely void of grass. Instead of a lawn, this yard is crammed to overflowing with shoulder-high coneflowers. It is only a small yard, but the flowers are so tall and the yard is so full of them that you get the feeling if you stepped off the sidewalk and in among them, as I'm often tempted to do, you would disappear and have to push your way through them for hours before you found your way out.

These, of course, are among the best days for walking because all the stuff in these gardens is slowly embracing autumnal colours, the golds and purples that give a rich sense of natural rhythm to the neighbourhood that lawns can't offer.

I don't hate grass. But I like the new way of growing it more than the old. There is a woman who lives not far from me who is still growing grass, but she's doing it with reckless abandon. She has a yard of grass, but it isn't Kentucky bluegrass, and it isn't cut as short as a toothbrush. The grass in her yard is exuberant grass, as tall as the grass on the prairie before the white man arrived. These days it is seven feet tall, with sprays of russet and pink flower heads that will, over the next few weeks, bleach out into bits of straw and eventually be smashed to the ground by the November rains. Another reminder of the rhythms of nature. If you walk by her house when there is a breeze blowing, her lawn rustles like tree leaves, or if you pass in the late afternoon, and it is backlit by the sun, you can see her grass arching up, the seed heads spraying out like a fountain. The effect is gorgeous, although I wonder if Olmsted walked by one night he might just consider it a mess.

31 September 2000

KISSING CONTEST

I was walking along Queen Street on a Friday afternoon not long ago when I spotted a crowd in front of the Mexx clothing store.

I am a sucker for crowds. It is a journalistic affliction. If there are fire engines, I follow. And if people have gathered up, I need to know *what* they have gathered up about. Put *me* at the back of a crowd, any crowd, and rather than walk away, I am doomed to work my lemming feet right to the front.

At the front of *this* crowd were seven largely immobile couples, embracing in the store window. *Living mannequins*, I thought to myself. *What's the big deal?* I was about to file the event under *old news* and move on when I spotted a big clock on the sidewalk keeping digital count of the hours, minutes and seconds. I wondered if maybe something grander was afoot.

"What's going on?" I asked the man on the bike beside me.

"They are trying to set a record for the longest kiss in the world," said the man.

Well, not so fast then. I had just stumbled on an event sanctioned by the *Guinness Book of World Records*. First time for that. And never having been present for a world record of *any* kind, Guinness or other, I decided I would stick around for a while.

The *first* thing I learned was that if I was going to be present for the record-setting moment, I might need more endurance than I was able to give.

It turns out the record for the longest kiss in the world, or the longest kiss Guinness has recognized anyway, was set by an English couple. But before I tell you how long *they* kissed, I should tell you the rules.

To qualify as the record-breaker, the kissers in the Mexx window would have to kiss continuously, which meant their lips couldn't part, not for even the briefest moment (you might want to check out your personal claustrophobia index here), *and* they would have to stay awake *and* vertical (they weren't allowed to lean on anything). If they needed to go to the bathroom, they *could* go, but only under a nurse's supervision (there was a nurse standing by). Even in the bathroom, however, their lips couldn't part. If their lips parted, they would be disqualified.

So using those rules, what do you think the record is for the longest kiss in the world? Or the one Guinness knows about anyway?

Who guessed … thirty-one hours, thirty minutes and thirty seconds?

"How long have they been going?" I asked the guy on the bike beside me.

The guy pointed to the clock on the sidewalk. "Twenty minutes," he said.

I decided to hang around. Before long I had made friends

with a clerk at the store who told me he and the other clerks had a pool going.

"I have totally lost," he said. "I predicted the first couple would drop out after five or ten minutes."

The first couple didn't go down until the two-hour mark—disqualified when the boy was caught leaning on a railing.

The second couple went around supper. They quit because the girl had to leave to pick up her sixteen-year-old sister from work.

And that left five couples in the running, and they had been running, or, more to the point, swaying back and forth, massaging each other's shoulders and backs, and wiping each other's chins with Kleenex, for about six hours. Which is when things started getting serious.

Before the contest began, they had agreed on a series of hand signals that they could use if they needed attention. Pointing at their mouths meant they were thirsty. (They were allowed to drink through straws as long as they kept lip contact.) Waving their fingers in the air above their heads meant they wanted to change positions, say to get out of the sun and into the shade. And pointing at the vicinity of their hips meant they needed to go the bathroom.

Marie-Claude and her husband, Jean, were the third couple to drop out. They had arrived believing they were a shoo-in for the $10,000 prize. Marie-Claude had misread the rules. She thought the world record was a thirty-*minute* kiss, not thirty hours. She and Jean figured they would have the prize in their pockets in a not unpleasant forty-five minutes.

"When we got to the eight-hour mark," said Marie-Claude, "we decided we would give it another two hours.

We decided if we hadn't won by then, we would call it a day."

And that brought us to ten o'clock on that Friday night. At ten, there were four couples left.

My favourite was the youngest: Matt and Taralyn, a couple in their early twenties who were both unbearably cute and who had been holding on to each other for dear life all day, sometimes with their eyes shut, and sometimes with their eyes wide open. They looked like a pair of little animals who could have happily cuddled up for an entire winter.

They were facing stiff competition. David Lindsay and his wife, Lin, for instance—they gave me the feeling they had done this before. They arrived with a supply of protein drinks, a notepad that they were using to write notes back and forth, and a newspaper that David was occasionally reading over Lin's shoulder.

I watched them for most of the afternoon, and then I took a break. I went back after supper for a spell and then again around midnight. By midnight, the guys, who had all arrived cleanly shaven that morning, were beginning to sprout stubble on their faces, which was presenting a problem. If you are a girl, and you have your face smashed up against a boy's face, and have had it there for twelve hours, stubble begins to hurt. In fact, it can feel, I am told, like you are being poked by a sharp stick. More than one stick, apparently.

So at midnight, when I called it a day, things were getting intense. The store had the feel of one of those Depression-era dance marathons; the couples kept shifting their feet, stretching, fidgeting, swaying, massaging and, of course, kissing. They were uncomfortable, no doubt about it. But they all seemed determined. Me too. Determined to get some sleep. I went home to bed.

I swung by early the next morning on my way to the market to find the crowds gone and, sadly, the contestants too. The only people in the store were a couple of tired sales staff sweeping up.

None of the couples beat the world record. Somewhere in the middle of the night, while I was sleeping, after fifteen hours and thirty-one minutes of kissing, a little over halfway to the record, a note circulated between the four couples, and they negotiated an end with a certain collective dignity. In a quintessentially Canadian way, they agreed to stop kissing together, combine first and second prize, and split the $12,000 worth of merchandise four ways.

That was around four in the morning.

Later in the week, the Guinness people announced they would include the Canadian couples in this year's record book for longest kiss in a storefront window.

We all know, of course, that people will do just about anything for fame and fortune. And people will stop and stare at the most awful things. At accidents, and fires, and fights. And it pleases me to remember that sweet afternoon this summer when I stumbled on the window of boys and girls who were trying to kiss their way into the limelight. I like to think that Taralyn and Matt are kissing now, snuggled up together, safe and sound, their eyes shut tight, the rest of the world, with all its sadness and sorrow, far away.

9 September 2007

SMALL DECISIONS

I have a friend, a woman who I don't see nearly enough. She lives in another city. I am always delighted when we collide. She is someone I have admired for years, for her sense of humour, and her joie de vivre, but also for the serious side of her. She is a busy woman, a professional, a person who *gets things done*, at work and, well, just about everywhere else too. She makes time to exercise every day, entertain at night and dress smartly. Her house is cleaner, and neater, and more organized than, well, than my house for sure.

She is the type of woman who writes thank-you notes. In fact, she is maddeningly perfect. Your life, or my life anyway, is hopelessly disorganized measured against hers. And I guess that's why I like her, because we are opposites, my friend and I, and you know what they say about that.

My friend has a touch of obsessive-compulsive disorder in her. That is not meant as a criticism. It doesn't get in the way of her life one little bit. If anything, it adds to it. She lives in the details, and that is why she gets so much done.

When faced with a big decision, or even a small one, my friend is likely to make a list of *pros* and *cons*. She thinks everything through as carefully as she can and considers *all* the possible implications and complications.

I ran into her recently and I could see that something was bothering her. I asked what it was, and pretty soon she was pouring out her heart. It turns out my friend went to a dinner party a few years ago and met a man who has recently become her fiancé. She realizes that this was the biggest thing that has happened to her in the last—well, probably in the last decade—and what has been bothering her is that she hadn't planned it out. Not one little bit. She just went to dinner, no list, no thought, no pros, no cons, no hemming and hawing, and *wham-o*! she is going to get married. Something she had never planned on or expected.

I know someone else who recently moved from the city to the country, radically changing his life. I asked him how things were going, and he said he wasn't sure.

"I changed *everything* when I moved," he said. "I used to live in the heart of downtown. I went out every night. Now that I live in the country, I stay home all the time. I have to *drive* to go to town. And when I get there, there is nothing around, except a corner store. In the city I *walked* everywhere. Now I have to get in my car to get my mail. I have changed *everything*, yet I feel like I haven't changed a thing."

He shook his head and looked at me. "Everything has changed, but it all feels the same. I didn't think it would be like this."

Those two conversations got me thinking. It is rarely the big decisions that affect us. It is, more often than not, the little ones.

We sit there sweating over the list of pros and cons, about

whether we should live in the country or the city, buy the Apple or the PC, take *this* job or *that* one. We fret, and agonize, and come to terms with what we think, and then fret some more, and change our minds, and then, finally, we take a big deep breath and come downstairs one morning and announce what we are going to do. And we think it is so big, and important, and monumental, and earth-shattering. And it isn't. Not one little bit. *Everything* changes and then—*nothing* changes.

It is never the move to the country or the decision to have kids that changes everything. It is the dinner parties. The little things that you didn't think twice about. It is the girl you sit beside on the bus without even noticing—the bus ride you took on a whim.

The big things, it turns out, are in the small things—the ones you can neither prepare for nor plan.

And what should we do about that? Nothing, it seems. Mostly, I think, it means we should relax and go with the flow or, better, with our hearts. Our hearts know the way, and the trick, it seems, is to follow our hearts. Because if we do, everything will work out all right in the end. And if doesn't? Well, you know the answer to that. That just means it's not the end.

15 February 2009

SILENCE

I was asked by a kindergarten teacher if I would read to the boys in her classroom.

"The entire class is boys this year," she said, then added, "Don't ask me to explain the probability of that."

She said she was having a problem with her all-boy kindergarten. "It's hard getting them interested in reading," she said. "I am trying to find role models."

"How about the fathers?" I suggested.

"I have asked the fathers," she said. "Only one agreed to come in."

So it was that I found myself sitting on a miniature chair, about to introduce myself to fifteen little boys. The boys were sitting on the floor around me. As I was about to begin, I took a measure of their attention spans and thought, *I better involve them in this or I am going to lose them fast.*

I put my book down.

I said, "I want you to stand up, one after another, and look me in the eye and tell me your name."

It was the best I could come up with on the spur of the moment.

And so the boys began. One after the other they struggled up and looked me in the eye.

"I'm Charles."

"I'm Peter."

"I'm Duncan."

Until a little boy in a blue sweatshirt stood up, stared at me and didn't say a word.

"Would you like to whisper your name?" I asked.

The boy in the blue sweatshirt came and stood beside me. But he didn't open his mouth. He didn't say a word. His buddies came to his rescue.

"He's shy," said several of the boys at once.

"His name is Toby," added a couple of others.

"Why don't you put your mouth beside my ear and think your name," I said to the boy.

The boy put his mouth beside my ear. He still didn't say anything.

"Thank you," I said. "That was very good."

He went back to his place and sat down.

I was in that class for maybe half an hour before I said goodbye. I never actually read one of my stories. I told them an abridged version of one, and then I read them something by the children's author Robert Munsch.

During the half an hour I asked them a lot of questions. I did my best to involve them. Mostly I was trying my best to get the kid in the blue sweatshirt to say something. To tell the truth, getting Toby to say something became my entire focus. However, whenever I had him in my sights, one of the other boys came to his rescue.

"I really wanted Toby to say something," I said to the teacher as we were saying goodbye.

She shook her head. "Toby hasn't talked to me all year," she said. "He talks to the other boys, but he doesn't talk to adults. Toby is a selective mute."

Then she said, "He wouldn't even look at me at the beginning of the year. But he looks right at me now. I can tell he wants to talk. Sometimes I ask him to point at something and his arm will start to shake and he has to hold it to stop himself."

I had never heard of such a thing before.

What amazes me about Toby is this: he has elected to turn his back on the people most children rely on. He has decided not to talk to adults. To the children around him, this must seem like a magical defiance. Yet it has also made them insiders in a world where everyone else is out. Toby has given his classmates great power, for only they have the honour of his confidence, only they can speak to and for him. His world is the world of children. The rest of the children know that and apparently love him for it.

I have no idea what painful thing, big or little, Toby has seen, or experienced, that makes him distrust adults. I hope, as the years roll along, with the support and patience he seems to be getting, Toby will discover that the world can be a safe place.

I have thought a lot about Toby, and the boys in his class who have surrounded him with their innocent acceptance. I have wondered if the boys I grew up with would have been so accepting. I don't think so. We were a pretty unforgiving lot. I have wondered about our acceptance and forgiveness of difference today, in our offices and homes. And I have wondered how the boys in Toby's class will do as they leave the kingdom of childhood.

We all know children are capable of astounding acts of cruelty.

But they have an astonishing capacity for love and trust. They are capable of great kindness and sensitivity. And sometimes when you are permitted to see that, as I was in that kindergarten, it can restore your faith in humanity. And challenge you to be better.

25 March 2007

GEORGE LEARNS
TO SWIM

There was a small moment of triumph last Wednesday evening in the swimming pool at the Trinity Community Recreation Centre in downtown Toronto. George Foires climbed into the pool in the shallow end and, holding a flutter board tightly, kicked his way from one end of the pool to the other. When George finished, he beamed at his teacher, and then at his wife, Paula, who was watching from the gallery. George is thirty-six years old. It has taken him nine weeks of swimming lessons to develop the courage to make a trip the length of the pool without stopping and grabbing for the edge.

"When I was five years old," said George, "I went with my parents on a family vacation to Portugal. We went to the small village of Serra d'El Rei, north of Lisbon. One afternoon my father took me to the beach. I remember him grabbing me by the arms and carrying me out into the ocean. The water was as deep as his chest. I was terrified. I was screaming and kicking, but he held me there, and the waves hit my face, and I have been afraid of water ever since."

George has been so afraid of water that he can't remember the last time he took a bath. George takes showers. He is terrified of getting water on his face.

"If there is water on my face," he says, "I can't breathe. I am afraid I am going to inhale the water and drown. Just to have water on my face makes me feel like I am suffocating. If I get water on my face, I have to hang on to something and I have to wipe the water off. Immediately."

When George was a teenager everyone would go to the beach. He would go too, but he wouldn't go in the water.

"I would watch," he says.

It used to scare him the most when he had to watch his brother.

"It was awful. I would say to him, 'Do you have to go so far out? Do you have to go so deep?' I hated watching him. I always thought he was going to drown.

"I couldn't wait for him to come out of the water."

Sometimes George would take his shoes off and go in as far as his ankles. But if he saw a wave coming, he would panic and get out.

"You try to hide it," he says, "but you can't hide it. You try not to talk about it. It is embarrassing."

Then ten years ago George's worst nightmare actually happened.

George has a friend who has a swimming pool in his backyard. George was at his friend's home for a barbecue. He was sitting on the patio, as he always did, as far as possible from the pool. He was watching the water when he saw a little girl who was in the water start to drown.

"I could see the panic in her eyes," said George. "I jumped up, and ran to the edge, and I pulled her out. I actually saved someone.

"That just made it worse. I would think of that little girl

over and over. I would have dreams of her drowning. In the dreams she would change into my brother."

George is married, but he doesn't have any children of his own yet.

"My wife is thinking of getting pregnant," he says. "And I know that if we have kids, she is going to want to go on holidays."

It was while he was thinking of this that George resolved to overcome his fear. He signed up for lessons at his neighbourhood pool—every Wednesday night for nine weeks. He thought that he would be swimming after two or three weeks.

Learning to swim was harder than he thought. The first fear that he had to overcome was the fear of getting his face wet.

During the first class his instructor made him put his face in water.

"It was awful," says George. "I would duck down and then I would come out panicking, wiping the water out of my eyes."

By the end of the hour George wasn't sure he would come back. He began to have second thoughts.

"I began to think, Do I really need to know how to swim? Why change now?"

He went back.

During the second class he met a woman who was as frightened as he was.

"When I realized I was not the only person out there with a problem, that there were a lot of people like me, I thought, *If she can do this, I can do this too.* It made me resolute."

Then his instructor tried to get him to kick.

"She gave me a board and tried to get me to go from one end of the pool to the other. There is a line where the water gets deep. I couldn't make myself go past the line. I was afraid the board might slip out of my hands."

In the third class George's instructor taught him how to tread water.

"It was terrifying," says George. "I cannot describe the panic. I had four or five feet of water below me, and I tried, but every four or five seconds I had to reach out and touch the edge of the pool."

George went home and told Paula he was going to quit. Paula said, "You are doing fine. You should keep going."

George barely slept. He thought about it all night. He thought, *If she believes in me, I can do it.* So he went back.

George felt embarrassed in class because people who had started at the same time as him were already beginning to swim. He still was not swimming.

At the beginning of every session he goes to the shallow end and practises what he calls his *ritual.*

"I stand there by myself and put my face in the water and blow bubbles. I do it for about ten minutes. I have to teach myself each week that I can put my face in the water and not drown."

On the seventh week George skipped his ritual, and he panicked as soon as class began. So he went back to his ritual before every class. Last week he felt secure enough to venture into the deep end with his flutter board.

"For the first time," he said, "I knew that if it were to slip out of my hands, I wouldn't drown."

And when he finished, when he kicked from one end of the pool to the other, he smiled at his wife, who watches every week from the stands.

And that's when he knew, for the first time, that one day he would learn how to swim.

"I am very proud of myself," he said quietly on Thursday morning. "It is my dream to go south and go snorkelling with my wife in the Caribbean one winter."

Sometimes love calls us to do the most amazing things. Sometimes love calls us to be strong, and sometimes it calls us to put our strength away. And always where there is love, it will eventually call us to courage. It is a call that never comes without pain. A call that never comes easily. It comes in hospital rooms, and in living rooms, and it comes in class-rooms, and sometimes even in swimming pools.

24 March 2002

THE KEY

On 16 December 2008, a Sunday, I woke up to find the city where I live blanketed with snow. The snow had begun the previous evening. By that Sunday morning it had snowed so much and was snowing so heavily that we were, quite literally, up to our knees in snow, and apparently sinking deeper. At some point before noon, the police advised people to stay indoors unless they had urgent and necessary business. The city effectively shut down.

When that much snow is falling, especially when it is falling that fast, you don't want to let it build up too long. If you do, shovelling your walk and the sidewalk in front of your house, which is your civic responsibility where I live, can become a Herculean task. And so that morning, trying to stay on top of the situation, I ventured out a number of times with a shovel. On one of those trips, I began to think of a neighbour of mine. She was a close friend who had done a lot for me over the years, and she was not at home. She was, in fact, one of the few people who were actually *working* on that snowy Sunday.

This, I thought, was the perfect opportunity to repay her for the many thoughtful things she had done for me. I would shovel my walk and then walk over to her house and shovel hers.

My friend lives alone, but she has a tenant who lives in a basement apartment and comes and goes from the back of the house. The walk from the sidewalk to the back door is long, and snow usually drifts back there, so this would not be an insignificant favour. I was feeling, I don't mind saying, pretty good about myself for being so thoughtful and industrious. And then, as I began to do my walk, a man with a shovel, walking down the middle of my unplowed street, stopped and asked if I wanted his help.

"I'll do your walk for five dollars," he said.

Thinking more of my neighbour's *long* walk than my *short* one, I hired him.

While we shovelled, he told me a story. "I am down on my luck," he said. He told me he had just broken up with his wife and that he had put a down payment on an apartment, first and last month's rent, and when he showed up to move in, the man he had paid the deposit to had disappeared with his money.

"I was conned," he said. And that, he told me, was why he was staying at the hotel at the end of my street. The hotel at the end of my street is not the kind of place where you would choose to stay if you could help it. It is the kind of place you associate with people who are down on their luck. The man who was shovelling my walk then told me that he was a carpenter. "My wife is a doctor," he said.

You never know, when people tell you these kinds of stories, how much is true and how much is made up. I tended to believe him, though the doctor part made me wonder. In any case, it didn't matter. I wasn't inviting him *into* my house. I was paying him to shovel my walk. And now that I saw how hard he could work, to help me with my friend's.

When we got to her house, I saw that, just as I expected, the snow had drifted badly into the back walk. It was waist high at the back door. My friend's tenant was completely snowed in. *A good thing*, I thought to myself, *that I showed up.*

It took the two of us the better part of an hour to do the job, and I was feeling both tired and pleased when my friend showed up just as we finished. When she saw the clean walk, she said, "That's the nicest thing you have ever done for me."

I paid the man—more than I said I would pay him, probably more than I *should* have paid him, but it was almost Christmas, and he had worked hard, and maybe his story *was* true.

"That is too much money," said the man. And then, as if to give me my money's worth, he picked up a broom and set to work on my friend's front porch. Finishing touches. As we watched, he picked up the recycling bin, and the cedar chairs, and went at it. He was, it seemed, determined to remove every last fleck of snow.

Eventually he thanked me, and disappeared, and my friend and I chatted. Then I headed home too. It was, maybe, an hour later when my phone rang. It was my friend.

"We have a situation," she said.

She told me she had left a key to her front door under her recycling bin that morning. She said she had never done that before. She said she had left it there for her tenant, so she could come in and out through her front door because the back door was snowed in.

"It was there," she said, "when the man was sweeping." She had seen it when he lifted the bin. Now it was gone.

"I should have picked it up," she said, "but I didn't want to be suspicious of him just because he was hard up."

Then she said, "I have been looking for it for the past half-hour. I dug through all the snow. I didn't see it anywhere. Do you think he took it?"

My good deed wasn't looking so good anymore. And this is the part where *I* don't look so good.

I could have said, "I don't think that guy took the key. I will be right over. I will help you look for it." Or, "We could change the lock." I could have said all sorts of things. What I said was, "I will get your key back."

And I headed for the hotel where the man said he was staying.

I was feeling bad. I was feeling responsible. My friend is a young woman. And she lives alone. I was feeling that she was going to be scared in her house, and that was my fault.

She didn't have the key. I didn't have it. And she had looked through the snow. Where else could it be?

The hotel was a rougher place inside than it appeared from the street, the sort of place you might see in a movie about a drug bust. A Quentin Tarantino sort of place.

The sign said if you had any inquiries to go to room seven. The man in room seven said he had lent the guy in room twenty-four a shovel so he could earn some money. I went to room twenty-four. The man I had hired to help me answered the door.

It wasn't a big room. A single bed, a stained carpet, a desk, an old TV. There was no chair. He sat on the bed.

"I think you might have made a mistake," I said. "I think you might have picked up a key by mistake. I have come to get the key back."

I was trying to give him a way out. I didn't care about blame or retribution. I was convinced he had the key, or at least if he did, I wanted to make it easy for him to give it back.

He told me he didn't have a key. I told him it had been under the recycling bin. And now it wasn't.

"I wouldn't take a key," he said. "I wouldn't do that."

So then I told him I didn't know him, and that the room and the hotel didn't give him a lot of credibility or me a lot of comfort. I told him I needed comfort. He said he understood that.

He offered to show me some ID and pulled out his health card. I wrote down his ID numbers.

"If anything ever happened," I said.

"I understand," he replied.

And I went back to my friend's house.

"I don't think he has the key," I said. "And anyway, if he does, I think you're okay."

"I don't feel comfortable," said my friend. "I think I should change my lock. Just in case."

And so that is what we did.

It was Sunday, and it was late. We decided to wait until the next day. First thing Monday morning, my friend removed the lock and took it around the corner to a locksmith who rekeyed it. I was leaving town on business. As I was packing, my friend called. She couldn't get the lock reassembled. I had about forty-five minutes before I had to leave. I ran over. I couldn't reassemble it either. We called the locksmith. It took him about five minutes to get there and less than five to fix it. It wasn't a cheap morning. I paid for everything. It had turned into an expensive favour. But I figured we did the right thing. After all, the fellow at the hotel might have had the key.

Or maybe not.

"Maybe he didn't see it," I said. "Maybe he swept it away."

"Maybe," said my friend.

And that was more or less that. I felt foolish. I felt foolish that I had tried to do something good and that it turned into such a mess.

To be honest, I *wanted* to blame it on my friend. I wanted to say, *You should have picked that key up when he lifted the recycling bin and you saw it there.* I knew I shouldn't say that. And I didn't for a couple of weeks. But eventually, I did of course, and when I did, she said, "Yes, I know I should have picked it up, but I wanted to trust him."

And then she said the thing that *she* had been holding back. She said, "I wish you didn't bring him to my house." She said, "From now on, I don't want you bringing people like that to my house."

We both began to blame each other. But that's not what we wanted to do. The truth is we both just wished it hadn't happened.

Whenever we talked about it, we would end the conversation by agreeing that we did the right thing. We *had* to change the lock.

"We'll know for sure in the spring," said my friend.

It turns out we didn't have to wait until spring. We got our answer a week ago. There was a thaw. My friend found the key. The guy hadn't taken it. He had swept it off her porch.

I have been thinking about him ever since. I have a lot of questions.

Should I have brought him to her house in the first place? I still think yes.

Should my friend have picked up the key when she saw it? I think yes to this one too.

This is the hard one for me. Did I have any right to go to that hotel? By knocking on his door, I was accusing him of theft. Would I have done that if he had lived in a nice house? If he had a good job?

It bothers me to think that when I left him that afternoon, I might have left him feeling unfairly accused, or defeated. I think I would have felt that way if I was him, and I am sorry for that. Whatever it was that led him to that unfortunate hotel room, his life was hard enough.

I believe I owe him an apology. I went back to the hotel with the intention of delivering it. It was my intention to tell him that we had found the key and that he was off the hook. But he wasn't there anymore. On the off chance he reads this, I would like to say it anyway.

I am sorry that I doubted you.

27 January 2008

SAFE PLACES

Over the last fifty-odd years, the North American media—and I'm speaking of both the entertainment industry and the news bureaus that present the world to us—has framed our view of the world in a most unhelpful way. We've been told, over and over again, both directly and indirectly, that the world is not a safe place. A proposition I disagree with. This is not, I hasten to say, to imply that there aren't dangerous people in the world, or even dangerous states. It is a complex and complicated world, sometimes sad, and often frustrating, full of intrigue and intricacy; but the simple fact is we aren't surrounded by enemies, and the vast majority of people you might meet here, there or anywhere would lend a hand in help rather than in harm.

Yet the stories we're given in our movie theatres, on our televisions, and in our newspapers wouldn't lead us to this conclusion. Quite the opposite. Consider all the police shows, and reality shows, and talk shows. Look at the movie chosen by the Academy of Motion Pictures Arts and Sciences in 2008 as the best of the year, the best America could do—*No Country for Old Men*. It was a movie of unspeakable violence. It left me, anyway, with one lesson, which was to question my instinct to stop at the edge of a highway if I ever saw anyone in distress. That was one way the villain (or was it the hero?) would pose when he wanted to lay a trap for one of his many luckless victims.

We've bought this danger story hook, line and sinker, and in so doing, we've robbed our children of childhood. I fell for it too, which is probably why I feel so strongly about this.

The fact is that the strangers our schools teach children to avoid are more apt to help than to harm them. Yet we hover around our children like Secret Service agents shielding them from dangers that don't exist, and instead of sending them next door to call on a friend, we arrange play dates as if we were social secretaries rather than moms and dads.

It is worth pointing out that it's not just the media that should be held to account. Political leaders have been equally adept at this game. It has served more than one leader to paint the world as a dangerous place, to point to the enemies lurking around us. Here in Canada various politicians and police forces, serving their own self-interests, have warned us about rising crimes rates when quite the reverse is true.

Any person who has travelled widely would tell you this world is full of men and women just like you, men and women who are anxious to look after themselves, provide for their families and muddle through to the end as best they can. There are not armies huddled on our borders in the darkness, and if there are, they are the armies of the hungry and the dispossessed. And yes, again, there are bad guys, and yes, it is a tricky business navigating the ship of state, but any political leader who tries to tell you it's time to circle the wagons is trying to sell you a bill of goods.

And that's the truth.

It is not said enough, so I'll say it again: the world is a good place, full of good people, and when we act out of that, when we act out of hope, and optimism, and faith in our fellow human, we act out of our best selves, and we are capable of doing great things, and of contributing to the greater good.

Hope and optimism are not synonymous with naivety. We should be looking to the future with flinty and steely eyes, for sure, but they should be wide open with hope, not squinting in fear.

> Ask, and it shall be given you;
> Seek, and ye shall find;
> Knock, and it shall be opened unto you.

If it is evildoers you seek, you will find them aplenty; if it is enemies you want, they are there too. But if you want the truth, the truth is this: blessed are the peacemakers, for they will be called the children of God.

9 September 2008

THE GIRL WITH
THE GLOBE

I was on my way home from one of the many farmers' markets that dot the city in the summertime. My backseat was full of spinach and chard, pears and plums, old cheddar and fresh bread. I was driving slowly, wondering what I was going to eat first, and if the world ever got any better than this, when up ahead of me, it suddenly did. I spotted a young woman with the world literally on the back of her bike. She was pedalling in a random, summery way, without, it seemed to me, a care in the world. There was something fetching about her. Not *her* exactly. I couldn't *see* her, except for the back of her plaid shirt. It was the *picture* of this young woman, with a globe, one of the old spinning kind that they used to have in the corners of classrooms, stuffed precariously into the basket on her back fender.

I don't know why this image pleased me so. But it did. Enough that I rolled down my window when I caught up to her, smiled, and said, "Where did you get that?"

"Hey," she said. And she flashed me a smile. "I know who you are." So we stopped. Both of us. And I got out of my car. And she got off her bike. And we chatted for a while.

Her name was Madeleine. And she told me she was on her way back from the park, where she had been hanging out with her friend and his dog. And that on her way home she had spotted the globe in a pile of garbage on the side of the street.

"I always look in the garbage," she said. "My mom taught me that." She said that she saw the globe lying beside a broken computer chair, and a box of plates and old magazines, and some ripped plastic bags. And she told me when she saw it, she stopped, looked around and, when she was sure that no one wanted it, picked it up and put it on the back of her bike.

And ever since she had it back there, all the way home, she had been singing that old song, "He's Got the Whole World in His Hands."

"I was still singing when you pulled up beside me," she said.

So we went for a coffee and she told me about herself.

She told me life has not always been easy for her.

"I left home when I was fifteen," she said. "And I have never lived in one place for longer than six months. I am always moving. Until I got to the place where I live now. I have lived there for two years, and I love it. Now I have to leave *it* because my landlord is renovating, and he is kicking me out. And I have to decide where I am going to go next. I am thinking maybe Brooklyn, or Montreal, or Edmonton, or Kingston. I lived in Mexico for a while and nearly got married there. But that didn't work out."

And then she shrugged.

"Life is not always clear," she said.

And then she pointed at the globe.

"It is a great sign, though. Having a globe on your bike. Especially if you don't think life has been fair.

"You are thinking *that*, and then you find a globe, and for some reason it makes you feel like life is giving you a sign in a delightful kind of way.

"So no matter how confusing things are, or how set back you feel, you know, if you have a globe on the back of your bike, it is all good.

"I think it is the universe talking to me," she said. "It is telling me to go ahead and expose myself to change, and if I do that, something good will happen."

We sat in silence after that. A surprisingly comfortable silence for two people who had just met, and then she smiled and shrugged again and said, "That's all I can say. I don't know if this story has an ending."

And she got on her bike and pedalled away.

I watched her leave, and as I did, I felt like there were things I should have said. For instance, I should have said, *Everything is going to be all right. Nothing happens without a reason. You will be fine.* But I didn't know that. Sometimes things aren't fine. And, besides, she didn't need to hear that from me. Yes, she had some heavy lifting to do, but she had a globe on the back of her bike. And she was singing when we met. And singing too, I bet, as she pedalled away.

12 July 2009

TASTING NOTES

NEW YEAR'S EGGS

We all have our traditions to ring in the New Year. I have mine. One of them is to eat eggs for breakfast on New Year's morning. It is, I have been told, good luck to eat something round to welcome in the year, which is *my* good luck, because my little egg ritual began for a different reason all together. It started, abruptly, on a New Year's morning some thirty years ago and has been my tradition ever since. I remember that morning as clearly as if it happened yesterday.

I had spent many years *not* eating eggs. For a while it was a (misguided, I now learn) health thing. It didn't begin as a health thing, however. It began in the foggy mist of my youth, the way these things often begin with children, for determined yet unexplainable reasons.

To be truthful, I don't remember the specifics. I just know that I was a boy who ate eggs, and then, all of a sudden, I was a boy who didn't. When I *was* eating eggs, I mostly ate them soft boiled, with little toast soldiers lined up for dipping. In fact, I think we called them "dippy eggs" in my family. And I can remember I liked eggs enough for a while that I would request "dippy eggs" from time to time.

And then I went off them, for whatever reason that was. And

when I went off them, I went off them with a *vengeance*. I went off avocado too. Or I never started avocado. I think avocado was just becoming common in Canadian stores at the time. And when it arrived at my house, I somehow got avocado mixed up with eggplant. Understandably, because an avocado is the same shape as an egg and the flesh of an avocado looks suspiciously egglike. And that was all it took to put *me* off avocado. I was having nothing to do with eggs, and that meant I was having nothing to do with something as suspicious as an egg*plant,* no matter how often I was told that avocados weren't eggplants, and even if they were, eggplants had nothing to do with eggs. The avocado was doomed, collateral damage, sucked into the slipstream of my suspicion.

This, as I said, was back in boyhood. But as is the way with these things, behaviour became belief, and eventually I came to believe I hated eggs. And then that eggs were hateful. And avocados too, for that matter. I hated them through my adolescence and into my college years. Just the thought of eggs made me sick.

The point is that I wasn't eating eggs. And then one morning I woke up and right out of the blue decided fried eggs would be the most perfect breakfast I could imagine. As I recall, someone I admired had mentioned that fried eggs were *their* favourite thing in the world, and that was all it took. It happened to be New Year's morning.

I fried up some eggs and, surprise, surprise, I liked them. And now I eat eggs. And avocados. Sometimes two a day. Eggs, that is. And always on New Year's morning.

I was wondering about this the other morning as I made my traditional meal. This is the time of year where everyone talks about change: a change in diet, a change in routine, a change in resolution. A change in regime. We all, it seems to me, have the desire to change hardwired into our systems. And maybe our capacity is greater than we think. All it takes is a little courage, a little forgiveness and perhaps some buttery toast. Change often seems overwhelming. But it can happen.

Of all the things you can think about as we stumble into a new year, that is probably as good as anything.

13 January 2008

THE TALL GRASS PRAIRIE
BREAD COMPANY

We were going to Manitoba to record a show. Before we left for the airport, my friend and colleague Julie Penner stopped by my desk.

"When you get to Winnipeg," she said, "I want you to promise me that you will go to the Tall Grass Prairie Bread Company for breakfast. When you are there, say hi to Tabitha. She is one of the owners. I think you'd like her."

And so it was, a few days later, that I found myself sharing my breakfast with Tabitha Langel, who appeared from the back of the bakery covered in flour and sat at my table, drinking coffee while I ate.

Tabitha is a lapsed Hutterite. She left the Hutterite community where she grew up because she was curious. She moved to Winnipeg, married, settled down and joined an ecumenical church, a church that includes Mennonites, Hutterites, Lutherans, Presbyterians and some Catholics. The bakery was born out of conversations that began at the church.

The church members were wondering how they could be more of a community. Although most of them lived in the same neighbourhood, they were wondering if they could *work* together in some way too.

This was in the late 1980s, a time when grain farmers were getting the lowest grain prices Canada had ever seen—about two cents on a loaf of bread. Farmers were struggling. Farm suicides were at a record high. Another question that arose at church was if there was anything they could do to support farmers. That is when the idea of starting a bread co-op began—an idea they thought could address both concerns.

Tabitha and her church friends wondered that if they went to one farm, bought their grain directly, then milled the grain and baked the bread themselves, they could afford to pay *more* than the two-cent average. They would be supporting one farm family, having fun baking together and maybe even getting some decent bread out of the deal.

So they began. They rented a kitchen at the St. Margaret's Church and baked bread every Saturday night. Kids delivered the bread around the neighbourhood in little red wagons. And the co-op grew. Neighbourhood people joined. It became a community thing instead of a church thing. Anyone could work in the co-op and get work credits. People who were well off were invited to pay a little more for their bread to carry those who couldn't. After a few years they *were* actually supporting a family farm *and* having fun. Just as they had planned.

The success provoked *more* discussion. The discussion was wide-ranging. *What,* they wondered, *is good stewardship of land? And What does that mean to people who live in the city?* If you believed, as Tabitha and her friends did, that herbicides and pesticides were not God's best idea, *how should you proceed if you are city folk? How much should those who live in the city pay for grain if they want to behave ethically? What*

*would things look like if instead of having farmers beg city
people for pennies, city people beg farmers for grain?*

And *What could they do about any of this? Could they support
farmers in some larger way?*

They decided to open a bakery. They found one for sale
and figured they needed $40,000 to get it going. They went to
the bank. They explained they wanted to sell bread at two
dollars a loaf, rather than the going rate of fifty cents. The
bank said this was absurd. They told the bank manager that
if you explained to people that you were charging more so
you could pay farmers more, people would be happy to pay
the extra. The bank said that wasn't the way the world
worked. They didn't get any money from the bank.

They got money from friends instead—some low-interest
loans, some no-interest loans. They promised to pay the loans
back if, and when, they could.

They believed there was a great hunger for connection.
They believed that farmers wanted to meet the city people
who used their crops and that city people wanted to know
where their food came from.

They had no idea if they were right. Everyone told them
they weren't. Everyone told them they would fail. They
decided not to do anything in a grandiose way. For opening
day they baked thirty loaves of bread, two dozen muffins and
twelve cinnamon buns. When they opened their doors at ten
in the morning, there were two hundred people lined up at
the door.

They had planned to have a bread blessing, but after ten
minutes there was no bread left to bless. Someone gave their
loaf back and they blessed *it,* broke it and ate it.

They kept growing.

And growing.

They had made all these careful plans for failure. They had worked out how they might exist selling twelve loaves of bread a day. They hadn't given any thought to what happened if they were wildly successful.

It was a nightmare. They were working so hard. Tabitha remembers the day the timer on the oven went off and she picked up the phone and couldn't figure out why no one was saying hello.

Today, some fifteen years later, they have opened a second branch of their bakery. They still have the little hole in the wall in Wolseley, where it all began, and now they have added one at the Forks. They support five farm families and employ about fifty people. And they have learned that you can't get rich when you pay fair wages to both farmers and staff, but you can make a decent living.

"We buy our wild rice from a local native co-op," said Tabitha. "We could get it way cheaper elsewhere, but we like what these folks are doing. They have a store in the poorest part of the city and they won't sell cigarettes. They are part of changing *their* community. We want to support them."

She picked up her coffee and looked around her bakery and smiled. "If something is too cheap, that means someone is paying the cost somewhere. Maybe it is the environment, or maybe it is someone else down the line.

"The average food item in the average grocery store travels two thousand miles," she said. "Here, in the bakery, the average is two hundred miles.

"The farmers come here and deliver their grain. And they

see the bread. They see where their grain is going. And our customers see where it is coming from. They can have coffee together."

Tabitha says she has learned that if you're mindful of what you're doing, you *can* make a difference to the local economy.

"The questions that we continue to ask," she said, "are how we can be *more* local, *more* just, *more* environmentally conscious than we were yesterday.

"It has been an unbelievable journey," she continued. "I am honoured to be part of it. I am a tad tired. But show me a baker who isn't."

The Tall Grass Prairie Bread Company started in 1990 with two people on staff. They baked thirty loaves of bread on opening day. The Saturday I visited, they baked about seven hundred loaves of bread, all organic, and many hand-shaped. Tabitha didn't know how many cinnamon buns and croissants.

I am a lucky man. I get to travel all across this country and talk to people from coast to coast. Mostly I get to tell *my* stories, but often I get to hear others. This is one of my favourites.

11 June 2006

APPLE PEELING

I own, at last count, twelve kitchen appliances. To wit: a microwave, a toaster, a food processor, a Mixmaster, a coffee maker and, God help me, a George Foreman Grill—which came, like a Cracker Jack premium, packed inside the microwave, $34.50 for the two of them. I thought the *microwave* was a deal at $34.50. And six others.

Twelve appliances that I kept lined up on my kitchen counter, as if I was running a showroom, until the derision heaped upon me by my so-called friends, all of them women, passed a tipping point. Now I have packed up my counter of wonders, and my appliances are stored in various cupboards.

I kept them out on the assumption that I would never use them if I didn't see them. I finally accepted the fact that I didn't use them anyway, and I have to admit that I'm not unhappy with the new state of affairs. The clean counter space *is* more relaxing. And there is less chatter in my kitchen about the things that I'm not doing, like chopping or mixing, brewing or juicing. If the chatter is still ongoing, it is, at least, going on behind closed doors. As I do the things I do best in a kitchen, like throwing away food that has gone by, especially pears and bananas, it is at least unwitnessed by the juicer, which was silent, but you could tell what it was thinking. Or I could.

I did leave one appliance out. When the moment of truth arrived, I was unable to put away my candy-apple, green-flecked, apple-peeling machine. The only appliance out of the twelve that doesn't plug in.

I bought it when I was in university—a suction-based model, which you can use on any flat surface, as opposed to the screw-clamp model that requires a lip.

The apple-peeling machine is made out of cast iron and only has twenty-three parts, including the peeling blade, the thumb screw, the three-prong fork, the peeling arm and the wood handle grip, to name five of them. It does only one thing—peels and slices apples, automatically and perfectly. Actually, it does potatoes too, but although I have, in the years I have owned it, peeled hundreds, maybe even thousands of apples, I have never done a potato. I did try a pear once, but I wouldn't recommend it.

I don't know why the peeler pleases me so much. Maybe because I have owned it for nearly thirty years, and you can tell, just by looking at it, that it is good for *another* thirty. Or maybe I like it because all you have to do is stick an apple on the three-prong fork, turn the wooden handle and the apple skin peels off it in a perfect long and continuous ribbon. Then, as I learned when I was a boy, before you eat the apple, you can take the peel, throw it over your shoulder and it will fly through the air and land on the kitchen floor, forming the initial of your one true love. I always do that when I am finished peeling my apple. Over and over again for thirty years now.

23 January 2004

WATERMELON

The Elizabethans, I have read, used to believe in something they called a "world order." This was a formal and strict hierarchy of the world's beings and things, a hierarchy that "began with the angels and ended with the ants," everything carefully sorted from the top to bottom. Elizabethans, who didn't have Paris Hilton to preoccupy them, spent a lot of time arguing about the sorting, trying to arrive at a consensus of where every little and large thing fit, which might seem like a trivial pursuit to you but was important business to an Elizabethan, given the fact that they believed if anything ever moved *out* of its order—say, for instance, a peasant was to become a king—then the world would tumble into chaos.

In these democratic days we live in, the order of things has become more fluid. Relativism is the password of the era, and the idea there might be a world order we could all agree on has long faded to black. Or, more to the point, from the public to the private. Because, like it or not, we are all at heart Elizabethans. We go to the polling booth when we are called to, but deep in our souls we all carry around our private sense of where things fit in the world. But I would put forward that one of the true delights of life is those moments when your sense of order and where things fit is turned upside down. Which is why, of course, we all want to bet on the underdog or can't help watching when some holier-than-thou preacher is hoisted on his own petard.

A few weeks ago, as you have probably guessed by now, *my* sense of order was sent for a loop. I am still reeling. It came, as bad news so often does, or used to anyway, with the morning mail. An item in a magazine I subscribe to, a magazine whose job it is to keep me on the cutting edge of things. And in this issue, on the cutting edge of things nutritional.

The article was simple enough. The editors had developed a scale on which to rank and sort, according to their nutritional value, all the fruits of the world. Something any God-fearing Elizabethan would be happy to read about.

They used six variables, including the amount of vitamin C, fibre, potassium, folacin and those pesky little carotenoids. I settled down to study the results, and I'll admit it, I settled down a little smugly, thinking to myself, I know the answer to this. *The blueberry,* I thought, *is the most nutritious fruit in the world.*

Not even close. Blueberry ranked number 23 on the list, with a total score of 59, well behind all the gold-medal fruits like the mango, which got a score of 97, or the grapefruit, which came in at 110, or the cantaloupe at 204. Impressive, yes, but in a whole different universe than the winner, which scored 424 on the scale—who guessed guava?

Guava is not an answer that would ever have occurred to me. I haven't, to my knowledge, ever eaten a guava. Nor have

I examined one with curiosity in the produce section of my local grocer. I haven't eaten, haven't touched, haven't even seen a guava. To be honest, I wouldn't know a guava if it fell from a tree and hit me on the head, or rolled out from under a bush, or tumbled from a vine, or whatever guavas do.

But it didn't totally surprise me, it didn't shock me that something as strange, and rare, and exotic as a guava was the silver bullet of health; what knocked me for a loop was the fruit that came in second.

The fruit that edged out the grapefruit, and papaya, and the kiwi, and the cantaloupe, and the blackberry, and what am I saying? It didn't edge them out. It demolished them. The blackberry, for instance, which I had been thinking was a virtual antioxidant nuclear bomb, only scored 124 points on this scale. The fruit that came second place had 311 points. That's more than double. And the fruit that came in second place was *the watermelon*.

Don't get me wrong.

I love watermelon. But I have always felt it was no more than coloured sugar water. Nature's Kool-Aid, as it were. And now I read that two cups of watermelon have the same amount of fibre as two slices of pineapple. If you would have asked me a week ago, I would have told you the only way to get fibre from a watermelon would be to eat the rind. (Pineapple, by the way, received 47 nutritional points.) But watermelon's real boasting rights are its high levels of lycopene—a proven cancer-fighting agent.

There were other shockers on the list. The papaya outstripped the orange. Persimmons trumped bananas, and most shockingly, the apple, the apple of fame and folklore, came in a dismal 33rd in the rankings, after rhubarb, for heaven's sake.

And this was when my view of the world began to totter, and I began to wonder if maybe my entire food choice system was misguided. If I could be so wrong about watermelon, what other nutritional crimes was I committing out of ignorance?

Maybe I should be eating *more* doughnuts. Maybe two cups of coffee a day is *not* enough. Maybe I should have started smoking at fourteen like all my friends said.

All I can say with certainty is that it's pretty clear I haven't been eating enough watermelon—which is understandable.

It isn't the most convenient of fruits. You can't throw a slab of watermelon in your backpack in case you get hungry on your way to work. And it is a fridge hog. Even a modest watermelon will fill an entire fruit drawer, and not leave room for, well, even a guava. You pretty much have to own a car to transport a sizable watermelon home from the grocery store. You are not likely to pick one up on a whim when you are out for an evening stroll. Buying a watermelon, unlike, say, buying a nectarine (39 points), is a commitment.

And it isn't exactly versatile. You will not, in the depths of winter when fresh watermelons are scarce, find cans of watermelon chunks with the other canned fruits. There is no such thing as fresh frozen watermelon, or jars of watermelon sauce, homemade or otherwise. And I can't imagine the wretchedness of attempting to make, or eat, a watermelon pie. Furthermore, if there is such a thing as fresh squeezed, un-reconstituted watermelon juice, I have yet to hear of it.

At www.watermelon.org you can find the National Watermelon Promotion Board and download an impressive list of watermelon recipes if you feel so inclined—like grilled watermelon cheddar burgers or watermelon stir-fry with chicken and capers.

Misguided, I would say.

I would like to put forward that the watermelon's drawbacks are its strengths. They aren't shoved into every muffin or cake like the ubiquitous raisin. They are somewhat of a rarity. A transient portent of good things to come. A sign of summer. When huge cardboard boxes filled to the brim with the enormous, unlikely fruit show up in the grocery store, they signal the beginning of hot, lazy days. Like summer, melons are fleeting. Those boxes won't be there for long.

You have about two months to indulge in as much lycopene as you want. What are you waiting for?

As the famed tenor Enrico Caruso once said, "Watermelon. It's a good fruit. You eat, you drink, you wash your face."

12 June 2005

ODE TO THE POTATO

My ode to the potato,
that humble little tuber,
which looks like a hippopotamus
or something rather ruder
if you leave it in a bag, that is,
instead of in the pot,
and it goes all soft and wrinkly
and smells like stuff
I'd rather not talk about
while standing on this stage,
for the purpose of my little ode
is really to engage
your imagination,
and your taste buds,
I'm not here to nag.
I have come to praise potatoes
I'm not here to make you gag.

You can mash them, bash them, put them in a pot.
You can freeze them, or fry them,
you can eat them cold or hot.

They're not mentioned in the bible.
Yes, that makes some folks wary.
And they are high in glyco-alkaloids
and that can make them scary,
causing headaches, cramps, comas
and in rare cases death.
But there's something else they cause,
I should mention in this breath:
sheer delight
if you slice them long and thin
and fry them up in oil.
Oh, let the sin begin.

I am talking of the French fry,
sprinkled liberally with salt.
I would die for French fries.
Is there anyone who'd not?

The humble *pomme de terre,*
the apple of my eye,
drenched in dill and butter,
or a sour creamy sigh.
A generous bowl of gnocchi,
a steaming bowl of soup,
a loaf of bread,
potato head,
a most congenial root.

I knew a woman once who grew one in the shape of a duck. She was living with a certain man, who planted her potatoes for her that spring. But she had a new man living with her in the fall when it was time to dig her potatoes. As she watched him, through the kitchen window, working the garden, the clothes snapping on her clothesline in the wind, she thought to herself, Love can come and go but a potato ... is forever. *Oh yes, they endure. Endure indeed they do.*

On the plates of kings,
the potato sings
a creamy song of cheese,
a saucy song of succulence,
a crispy tune of cheer
of butter lakes,
potato cakes,
pepper grinders,
parsley flakes.
Or in a pot,
a peasant stew,
a fire of flickering meals,
the darkening night,
potato blight,
an Irish sigh,
a teary eye.

One potato, two potato, three potato, four.
Five potato, six potato, seven potato, more.
And out you must go as fast as your flipper
flapper floppers can carry you.

potato feast,
potato famine,
boiled alone,
scalloped with salmon,
my bud,
my spud,
my sweet potato pie,
my Yukon gold,
I'm growing old,
stay with me till I die

7 September 2008

THE BAY LEAF

I have harboured doubts about bay leaves for years. Whenever I have come across one (and I have pulled my fair share of bay leaves out of soups and stews), I have rolled my eyes, either literally or figuratively, privately or publicly, depending on the company, because, well, between you and me, I have never seen the point.

More to the point, the bay leaf is the only spice that has ever humiliated me. Surely I can't be the only one who has, on more than one occasion in my case, removed a piece of bay leaf from my mouth and signalled my wait staff, my plate pushed discreetly forward, my head dropped, as I stare at this thing I have worked out of my mouth. Then, as politely as I can manage given the circumstances, allowed that I wouldn't be finishing my soup or stew or whatever it was, having found this bit of *whatever* in it. I have handed the wet leaf over in my supercilious way, calculating all the while in my cold little heart the free meal I have undoubtedly scored, only to be told that that little bit of *whatever* wasn't *whatever* at all.

Maybe I *am* the only one who has done this?

But surely it is reasonable to harbour doubts, grave doubts, about a spice that can reasonably be confused with any number of things? Some of them plastic. A bay leaf doesn't seem to undergo any physical transformation even after bubbling in a pot of beef stew for literally hours—your beef is as tender as beef tends to get, and your bay leaf is still hard and plasticy enough for me to ... to, well, you know what I did.

It has long been my contention that the bay leaf hangs around the spice rack like a dim relative. The plumber's helper. The photographer's assistant. The vice-president of spices. The guy who doesn't seem to be doing anything at all but is on the payroll just in case. The placebo of the spice rack.

It has been my belief that a pot of stew *without* that bay leaf would taste no different, not at all, not one whiff, than the pot *with* it. Or for that matter, a pot full of them. Go ahead. Double up *whatever* the recipe calls for and tell me you can tell the difference.

Try that with garlic. (Garlic, which, incidentally, was worshipped by the Egyptians. And, I would put forward, with good reason.)

Or try that with cloves. Wars were fought over cloves. Cloves have played a pivotal part in world history.

Tradition tells us that thyme was in the straw bed of the Christ.

The only thing I know about bay leaves is that if you keep them in a dark place, they last for years, maybe even lifetimes, with no evidence of change.

Have you ever *tried* a bay leaf?

I did this week.

I had nothing better to do, and before I knew it, I was

standing in front of my spice rack, like a photographer's assistant, and something came over me ... guilt? Who knows.

Anyway, I popped one in my mouth, and I can report that slipping a bay leaf into your mouth and letting it marinate there, between your teeth and cheek, for, say, a half an hour, like I did the other afternoon, is not unlike walking on a piney mountaintop with the Aegean Sea stretched below you. At least I think it was the Aegean. It was an azure blue, that's for sure, and it smelled like pine, although there was also a distant scent of mint on the wind.

Bay leaves are, it turns out, flavourful in their dry Mediterranean way, and if you give them little nips with your teeth every so often, they release bursts of sappy flavour, not as strong as *pine* sap, more a memory of sap, with a tingling pineyness and hints of menthol. My leaf put me into a sort of Mediterranean ennui.

Before long, I was thinking how W.O. Mitchell was known for his snuff, and Mordecai Richler for those nasty little cigars, and wondering if maybe I should be known for something too. And why not for chewing bay leaves?

I could get a little silver box from Birks or, better, from the Bay, to carry my bay leaves around. A writer needs something like that to make him stick in the public's mind. And I'm not that big on snuff and cigars.

Perhaps a bay leaf isn't like the vice-president in charge of nothing in particular but is, instead, that fellow in the office with the indeterminate title, who despite being overlooked by just about everyone is really the person who gets everything done, who makes everyone else look good.

The Delphi oracle, I just read on the web, used to sniff the smoke of burning bay leaves to promote her visionary trances. There is a lot to read about the bay leaf if you do a little poking around. It turns out the bay leaf grows on the bay tree. And the bay tree is also known as the laurel tree, and the Greeks used to give laurel garlands to athletes at the Olympics. There is much, it turns out, to recommend bay. A baccalaureate means laurel of berries, and we have poet laureates, and well, bay leaves are my new thing.

I feel like I owe someone an apology.

18 May 2008

CHERRY SEASON 2006

The all-too-short 2006 cherry season has come and is almost gone where I live.

These days, when you can get a box of strawberries in the dead of winter, cherries may be the last of the seasonal fruit. They come, around here anyway, during the first few weeks in July.

And when they come, you know you have to move fast because by the time August arrives, cherries will be long gone. And you can mark me down in favour of that, in case you were wondering.

Not the going. But the *coming* and the going. I like to measure the passing of the years with things like that: the return of the warblers, the departure of the geese and, yes, our annual visit to the pick-your-own cherry orchard.

Cherries may be the most convivial of the summer fruits, the only fruit served communally. Strawberries require individual bowls. Put a single bowl of cherries on a table and one thing is for sure: people are going to hang around.

And what could be better than hanging around a bowl of cherries with your friends on a summer afternoon? Except maybe cherry-picking.

A cherry orchard may be the perfect place to while away some of the summer—like all orchards, it's blessed with the grace of shade; but unlike any other orchard I can think of, a grove of cherry trees has perfected the rhythm of summer. Which is to say that time in a cherry orchard moves languidly. You can pick more apples than you know what to do with in about five minutes. But a bucket of cherries can take hours, and that is about all the work that should be required of anyone on a sunny Sunday in July.

What could be better than to be sent out to the orchard and told not to come back until your bucket is full, and it is just you and that flock of starlings who are honing in on you like guided missiles, immune, apparently, to the banging of the propane bird clapper? The birds and the berries and the whir of the cicada and, of course, the red stain on your lips and fingers.

23 July 2006

READER'S
NOTES

BOOK BUYING

I moved, lock, stock and barrel, a year ago; over a year ago, come to think of it, and I still haven't unpacked the ten cartons of books that are in the basement. I haven't a hope of unpacking them until autumn at the earliest, and, let's be honest, that's not going to happen. I did go through the boxes at Christmas and pulled out the books I wanted to read first, and I have the ones that don't fit on the bookshelves stacked neatly, more or less, in piles in my bedroom and in the den, and there is a pile in the living room and one in the kitchen (but they are smaller piles), plus the ten boxes in the basement. They were heavy to carry down there. So, I've made myself a resolution, a firm and binding resolution that I'm not going to buy another book, not one, until I have read all the ones I have in the piles and gone through the ones in the basement.

Unless, of course, it is a book by Patrick O'Brian, who wrote the Aubrey/Maturin series, which *The New York Times* called the best historical novels ever written. Patrick O'Brian is exempt, that's fair, even though I've never read him before. Although I have started the first book, several times, and I didn't much like it, but I might start it again, and I might like those books this time. And if I do, I might finish the first four that I already own, and in case I do and want to read the next fifteen, I am allowed to buy them. So clearly I'm not including Patrick O'Brian.

And I'm allowed to buy a book if it's a book that I've already read and it's somewhere in the boxes in the basement and I want to reread it. I think you would agree it would be easier on everyone if I bought another copy rather than go into the basement and look for it. You can imagine what that would be like.

And it also doesn't count if the book is in the basement, or I think it's there, and I don't want to exactly *read* it but want it around so I can do any of the following things:

- consult it
- look at it
- have it on my shelf because it makes me feel better to have it there than to worry about it in the basement
- sell it to a second-hand bookstore
- lend it to a friend.

If it falls under any of those "special" circumstances or any other circumstances that I can't think of right now but might qualify as "special" at a later date, then I'm allowed to buy that book, even if I already own it and it's in the basement somewhere.

And I'm allowed to buy a book if I know it's a book that I might not necessarily read but need to have on my shelf because having it there might be helpful in some way that is hard to describe but has something to do with the phenomenon where you learn things just by being near them, like how you can learn a language by listening to tapes while you sleep—you go to sleep with the tape playing and you wake up and can speak the foreign language (as long as you're still able to speak your *own* language, because I don't want to wake up speaking Urdu if it means I have lost the ability to speak English).

And I'm allowed to buy books on subjects like losing weight, or meditation or any number of practical things like killing squirrels who ransack your garden or building a sauna in the woods. Those books are exempt. And I hardly think I have to list all the exempt categories because they are pretty obvious.

And I'm allowed to buy books if it's a book that more than one person says I should read, like say *five* people mention it. Okay, maybe five is a lot. Make it three people. And they don't necessarily have to tell *me* to read the book, but if they mention it in some way, even if they aren't speaking to me, then that should count. Like if I overhear them talking about the book at a dinner party. Or, say, see them reading the book on an airplane.

In the case of a book that has had a movie made about it, or won a major award, or appeared on a bestseller list, then less than three but more than one person.

And I'm allowed to buy a book if it was written by E.B. White or W.O. Mitchell or Margaret Wise Brown, even though I own everything by E.B. White already, but not in every edition, and there might be editions that are better than the ones I own, or even not as good, which might be good to have as backups, so everything by E.B. White is okay and isn't covered by this.

And if they discover something new by Shakespeare whose first name is strangely escaping me right now, or decide one way or another about *Double Falsehood*, even though I haven't read anything by Shakespeare since school, and even then I only read *Macbeth* and for the rest of them read the Coles notes or not even, if they discover a new Shakespeare, that is exempt because it might be the best one, and I wouldn't have to hear that from three people; in this case, one would do.

And first editions don't count.

Especially if it is by Shakespeare, but anyone else too.

I think that covers it.

3 June 2007

THE THOMAS FISHER
RARE BOOK LIBRARY

P.J. Carefoote is a librarian at the Thomas Fisher Rare Book Library at the University of Toronto. P.J. called to tell me he had a book he wanted to show me.

The Fisher Library is the largest rare book library in Canada. The collection includes clay tablets from 2000 B.C., papyrus scripts from the time of Christ and velum books from the Middle Ages.

It is housed in the odd-looking tower at the south end of the Robarts Library. From the outside, the Fisher appears to be stuck onto the end of the Robarts, like a figurehead on the prow of a Viking ship, albeit a concrete one. Inside, however, it's something else all together.

Walking into the Fisher is like entering a medieval cathedral. The light is dim and filtered, and the room (there is just one large room, a stunning six-storey atrium ringed by book-lined balconies) is, quite simply, breathtaking.

Umberto Eco spent time at the University of Toronto when he was working on his medieval mystery *The Name of the Rose*. Many believe the tower in his fictional fourteenth-century monastery owes much to the time Eco spent at the Fisher.

If it's a cathedral, however, it isn't a cathedral to the glory of God. It's a cathedral to literature and to the glory of man's struggle in the world of ideas. As you stand at the bottom of the atrium, in light so dim it could almost be candlelight, and look up at the thousands of leather-bound books, it is awe-inspiring to think that the library holds the collected sum total of human thought. It is, more than books, a collection of the ideas that men and women have considered worth preserving over the centuries.

Very little lasts for a century. Not many of our buildings last that long. But most of the books in the Fisher have been carefully preserved for *centuries upon centuries*.

I stood in the atrium, lost in the beauty of the place, when I realized P.J. was smiling at me.

"A lot of people do that," he said.

Then he said, "Come on." He took me upstairs onto the first balcony and pulled a huge volume off the shelf.

He held it out. A leather-bound volume that looked like an encyclopedia.

"The first folio," he said.

Published in 1623. The first printed collection of William Shakespeare's plays. It was put together by two of his fellow actors six years after his death. There are about one hundred copies left in the world. It was sold for a pound when it was printed and is worth about $6 million today.

"I have seen men cry when I have handed them this," said P.J. "This is where the art of the English language began. If this did not exist ..." P.J. shook his head. "Who knows?" he said.

He took the huge volume and began to flip through it.

"This one is called *The Rosebud Edition*," he said.

He flipped to page 395, the middle of the tragedy of *Cymbeline.* Someone had once used the book to press a rose. The oil from the flower had stained this page, leaving behind the perfect imprint of a rose.

"One of the lovely things about these books," said P.J., "is when you find something like this. A sign of everyday usage."

He put the book back and plucked another from farther down the shelf. "This is the Wicked Bible," he said. "There are only eleven of *these* in the world."

Having the right to print bibles in the late sixteenth and early seventeenth centuries was a licence to print money. Robert Barker's family had held the rights to print English bibles since the Elizabethan period. Rival printer Bonham Norton was jealous of the Barkers and their lucrative position. One night in 1631, he had one of his "printer's devils" sneak into Barker's print shop to mess with the type. The apprentice removed the word *not* from one of the commandments. When the bible was printed it read "thou *shalt* commit adultery."

It was a huge scandal. Barker was fined, and Norton, sadly, I would have to say (me being a man who has perpetrated worse jokes), had to reimburse Barker his fine.

P.J. took the bible and put it back on the shelf. He had more he wanted to show me.

"*This* is why you're here," he said.

He was holding out a leather-bound volume about the size of a large theatre program. The ninth edition of Gray's "Elegy Written in a Country Churchyard."

"Not a particularly interesting printing in itself," said P.J. "But it is, nevertheless, one of the most interesting books in

Canada. Because this copy once belonged to General James Wolfe."

He handed it to me.

Then he said, "We know Wolfe had this with him in Quebec. And from certain accounts, we believe that he was reading from it the night before the battle of the Plains of Abraham."

I was barely paying attention. I was holding in my hands the very book that James Wolfe had once held.

P.J. smiled. "That's not the most interesting thing," he said. "The most interesting thing is that he wrote in it."

I opened the book carefully. It was inscribed. *From KL ... Neptune at sea.*

The Neptune was the warship Wolfe sailed on. *KL* was Katherine Lowther, his fiancée.

I had never considered that General James Wolfe might have had a girlfriend.

I began to flip through the book. A few pages in, I stopped.

Wolfe had underlined the word *weary.* And again, *drowsy.*

I was looking for the poem's most famous line.

"The paths of glory lead but to the grave."

Each word was underlined individually.

It is said that the night before the battle, as he floated down the river, Wolfe quoted that line and said he would rather have written it than take Quebec.

There are four notes in the margins of the book, all in Wolfe's neat and precise hand.

P.J. said, "Most people don't like it when you write in books. I encourage it."

He shrugged. "A clean copy is beautiful, but it is more

beautiful to know what another reader was thinking while he was moving ahead of you.

"When you write in a book, it is like leaving your testimony for other readers. People who will never know you but will know your thoughts."

He nodded at the book I was holding. "Little notes like that are a reminder that these books belonged to someone else before they came here."

I handed Wolfe's book back to P.J.

As he walked me to the door, he said, "We are always looking for the sacredness beyond humanity."

Then he said, "I would posit that there is something sacred about these books. There are books here that have been censored and banned. There are books that are *not* here because they didn't survive."

The library is not just a testimony to the books. It is a testimony to the people who wanted them preserved. Looking after them is a sacred trust.

P.J. waved his arm around. "People wanted all this saved. These books meant something to them. They are witnesses to those who went before us. They have existed for hundreds of years. This is a holy place."

A secular kind of holy, perhaps. And yet the farther back you go, the more tangled it becomes, the harder to unknot the one from the other. Monks and nuns were once, quite literally, the keepers of knowledge: copying manuscripts and protecting them from harm. Now it is up to the librarians and those of us who support them in their sacred work.

5 October 2008

W.O. MITCHELL

My first job at the CBC was as a researcher on the national call-in show *Cross Country Checkup*. The first week I worked there, we did a show—prophetically, it turned out—on the death of the Eaton's catalogue. *What,* we asked Canadians, *did the Eaton's catalogue mean to you?* As hard as that is to imagine today, it meant a lot to many people. One of those people was the much-loved prairie writer W.O. Mitchell. *Cross Country Checkup* always has a few callers like Mitchell up their sleeve, standing by during the show to prime the pump. It was my job that week to call Bill Mitchell and book him.

I couldn't believe my luck. It was my first day on the job and I got to call W.O. Mitchell at home. That was the first time I spoke to his wife, Merna. You always spoke to Merna when you phoned the Mitchells, regardless of whether she got on the line, because when you spoke to Bill, it was always a three-way conversation, Bill holding the receiver and Merna orbiting around it.

Bill agreed to do a bit for *Checkup* and, in the course of our conversation, invited me to attend the premiere of his play *Back to Beulah,* which was opening a few weeks later at the Tarragon Theatre in Toronto.

"You should come," he said.

Well, of course, I did. Are you kidding? I had an invitation from Bill Mitchell himself, who, I imagined, would welcome me like a ... friend? Colleague? Who knows what I imagined. I bought a ticket and flew to Toronto from Montreal as if I had been summoned to Buckingham Palace by the Queen herself. I didn't understand that Bill hadn't expected me to follow up on the invitation and had forgotten it the moment he offered.

Bill was capable of that sort of thing, out of generosity, not malice. Pierre Berton was once invited to dinner at the Mitchells' and arrived a little late. Pierre met Bob Needham sitting glumly on the Mitchells' front porch.

"I think the fire is out," said Needham. The Mitchell kids had set the house on fire. But Merna and Bill were nowhere to be seen.

"Bill is out looking for Merna," said Bob.

Several hours earlier Bill had driven Merna ... well, that was the problem. He had driven her somewhere, and he had promised to pick her up and return her home so she could cook dinner for Pierre Berton and Bob Needham. The problem was Bill couldn't remember *where* it was he had dropped her and, thus, where it was he should pick her up. He thought it was possible he had taken her to the doctor. But it could have been the dentist. So while his house was burning cheerfully, Bill was driving around the city, with his head out the car window, bawling his wife's name, while Merna, who was standing in front of the medical building where she was supposed to be standing, tried to convince the police she wasn't a hooker. Meanwhile, Berton, who was still waiting on the front porch, watched while an unfamiliar woman with a suitcase burst out of the house.

"I can't stay here any longer," she announced on her way past him. It was Merna's mother.

I now know these sorts of moments to be the common stuff of Bill's life, but I didn't know that the weekend I appeared in Toronto, expecting to attend the opening of his play as his special guest. And I was shaken to get there and learn not only was there no ticket waiting for me at the box office, but the people in the box office had no idea I was coming. The theatre, of course, was sold out.

The box office staff took pity on me and put a bridge chair in an aisle. I saw the play, but I never saw Bill, and I left feeling a little special and a lot stood up.

Almost a decade passed before I met Bill again. The next time our paths crossed, I had moved to Toronto and was working at the old CBC Radio building on Jarvis Street. It was a late autumn afternoon when I came out of the building and saw him standing alone in the parking lot looking lost. Mostly in your life you don't do what I did next. Mostly you don't do those things you want to do with people you admire, or are attracted to, or love, which pretty much describes the way I felt about Bill. Mostly you think these things, but you let them go. That afternoon I didn't. Instead of walking away, and wondering about him, I walked up to W.O. Mitchell and introduced myself.

"We spoke years ago," I said. And then I heard myself inviting him home for dinner. "I have ball tickets," I said. "You could come to dinner and after we could go to the ball game."

I didn't know he was a big ball fan. I didn't know I was

making an offer he couldn't refuse. He lit up. But first we had to go to his hotel room to fetch a jacket and dump his briefcase.

He had a room directly across the street at the old Hampton Court Motel. When I prepared to step out onto Jarvis Street in the middle of the block, Bill shyly pulled me back. He pointed south to the corner of Carlton, where there was a traffic light.

"I promised Merna I would cross at the corner," he said.

That he would both make, and then keep, that promise speaks of the relationship he and Merna shared.

At dinner he held my young son in his lap. At the ball game he kept saying, "I wish Merna was here. She would like this so much."

That night was the beginning of our friendship. For the next twenty years we got together whenever our orbits collided.

Once, in Winnipeg, when we were both on a book tour, I was ushered into a radio station for an interview to find him sitting in the lobby, having already done his. He wasn't actually sitting; he had dropped onto a sofa in exhaustion and had slid so deeply into it he was almost horizontal. I had to step over his legs to get by him. It was another autumn afternoon, this time rainy, and windy, and cold. He was only wearing a thin beige trench coat. There was snuff sprinkled over the coat as if someone had seasoned him with cinnamon.

He is too old and too thinly dressed for this, I thought.

"Stuart," he said, opening one eye. "Is that you?"

I smiled.

"They're passing me around the country like a goddamn baton," he said. "Do you want to have dinner?"

He was reading that day, at lunchtime, to the Canadian Club. At his invitation, I once again watched him perform, this time from the back of the room. He had attracted a crowd of maybe five hundred enthusiastic fans, and faced with their enthusiasm, he came wonderfully alive. I attracted about fifty to my afternoon signing. At dinner I told him I was jealous.

Another time I took my two boys to a now defunct Toronto bookstore where he was signing copies of *Roses Are Difficult Here*. I wanted them to meet him. I wanted them to understand he was someone I thought was important. We stood in line, and appearing like that out of the blue, I wasn't sure he would recognize me. He did. He snatched the book out of my hand and explained in a voice everyone in the bookstore could hear that he had fought with his editor, my friend Doug Gibson, over a passage.

"First time Dougie and I ever fought," he said loudly.

During the editing Doug had made him clean up a phrase. He was still stewing about it.

It was, it turned out, the punchline to his story about the Christmas parade in the fictional foothills town of Shelby, Alberta. The way Mitchell wrote it, Canon Midford had organized the parade and had made the obvious choice for who should play Santa Claus: Art Ulmer. Sober.

It was Rory Napoleon's idea to take the antlers that hung on the wall behind the Arlington Arms reception counter—elk—and strap them to the pair of two-year-old bays that would haul Santa into town. In his shoe and harness shop,

Willie MacCrimmon fashioned special horn-holding bridles for the barely broken bays.

Everything worked as planned, until the reindeer bridles Willie MacCrimmon had made slid down and over the horses' noses on their way into town. They formed, as Mitchell told it, a sort of elk horn necklace that bumped alarmingly against the horses' chests and spooked them. By the time they got to the town square, where every child in Shelby was waiting with their parents, Santa's sleigh was wildly out of control, snort clouds of steam puffing from the horses' nostrils as they dragged the wild-eyed Santa past the review stand at a gallop.

"Whoa, you bay bastards," screamed Santa's driver on the page, as printed by McClelland & Stewart.

In the bookstore, Mitchell scowled. He looked at my boys and then at me. Then he picked up a pen and crossed the words out. With a flourish, he then replaced them with the words Doug Gibson had removed. Now Santa flew by the assembled families of Shelby, and my sons, screaming, "Whoa, you cocksuckers."

The bookseller looked uncomfortable. Bill squinted at her and shrugged. Then he winked at my boys and nodded at me. "Ah, shit," he said. "They live with him. They've heard worse than that. Haven't you, boys."

It wasn't a question.

I began to visit him whenever I found myself in Calgary. In the late autumn of 1995, I was in Calgary on another book tour, scheduled for an evening reading at the Memorial Park Library.

The organizers had done me the courtesy of booking a small room so the few people who had come were spilling into the aisles, making it appear as if there was almost a crowd. As I stood behind the lectern and surveyed my audience, there were Bill and Merna Mitchell sitting in the front row. I stepped around the podium and leaned over Bill, and he hugged me and gave me a kiss.

"I wouldn't do this for just anybody," he said. He meant come out for the reading.

I didn't know how sick he was. I went back to his house afterwards and found him in a wheelchair, wearing a bib, which he had managed to cover with snuff.

I began to phone every few weeks. Sometimes he didn't feel well enough for the phone, and I talked to Merna. Sometimes I phoned Doug Gibson for an update.

They both died within a few months of each other. I understand how Merna would have found it hard to go on without him. I miss him, and I think of him often—of the things he wrote, the things he taught me about writing, and the permission he gave me, by his own example, to enjoy reading in public. But mostly it is him I miss. He made me laugh, and knowing he was there, and how seriously he took his business, made me feel it was all right to be serious about this business myself.

6 November 1999

THE ISLAND OF
NO ADULTS

Teaching a child how to read is an enterprise that is fraught with danger and something that should only be undertaken after careful thought.

Oh, you can *start* with flashcards and exercise books, but you won't stay there. Reading invariably leads to books, and reading books inevitably leads to knowledge, and there is no telling where knowledge is going to lead anyone.

Take my friend Leah, for instance. The spring Leah was eight years old she took a book out of her school library. The book, written by Carol Ryrie Brink, was called *Baby Island*. It is, says Leah, a child's adventure in the Enid Blyton tradition, one of those books in which a group of kids go off and have an adventure without any beastly grown-ups getting in the way. In Carol Brink's book, as Leah remembers it, a group of young girls end up on an island looking after a bunch of babies.

"There were goats on the island," said Leah by way of explaining how they might do that. "They milked the goats."

Sounds innocent enough. Well, by the time the end of June rolled around, the police were involved, and there was talk at Leah's school of pulling *Baby Island* from the library.

That's because it was *Baby Island* that gave eight-year-old Leah the notion that she and her best friend, Amy, should set off and seek their fortune.

"We'll walk to Brighton," Leah told Amy. "We'll get jobs."

Leah lived in Cobourg. Brighton was the next town over.

Amy's father raised rabbits. All that spring Leah and Amy held secret planning meetings in the rabbit hutch in Amy's backyard. They decided they should wait until the weather was warm enough to sleep outside before they ran away from home.

So they waited until June, and on a Friday in June they agreed to meet at the schoolyard, at the top of the slide, at the stroke of midnight. Leah's father had gone out that night and left her with a babysitter. While the babysitter was in the basement playing video-games, eight-year-old Leah loaded a garbage bag with food. Then she took her dad's hockey bag and filled it with clothes and stuffed animals and tapes and her stereo, and books, of course, which were what gave her the idea in the first place. Then she took the garbage bag and the hockey bag up to her bedroom and heaved them out her bedroom window. She was planning on following them herself until she saw what happened to the yogourt containers when they hit the ground, so she slipped out the front door instead. She dragged the two bags down the street to the schoolyard, and there was Amy, wearing a tiny knapsack on her back, waiting at the top of the slide just like they had agreed.

There was a park near Amy's house. There were some woods behind the park. They decided they would sleep in the park and follow the shore of Lake Ontario to Brighton the next morning. When they got to Brighton, they would get jobs as waitresses.

Leah had packed a sleeping bag. They set up camp in the woods. As they lay there, Amy got scared. And at some point in the middle of the night, when they heard Amy's dad calling her name, Amy started to cry.

Amy said, "I'm going home."

"I'm going to Brighton to become a waitress," said Leah.

Leah said, "You can go home, but you have to promise not to tell anyone where I am."

She swore Amy to secrecy.

Ten minutes later Amy was back with her dad.

"I was pretty determined," Leah told me years later. "I think her dad had to pick me up and throw me over his shoulder. I was convinced I didn't need any adults. I was also convinced that when I got home I would be in deep trouble, because I had taken so much food out of the fridge and now it was ruined."

There is no better landscape than the landscapes of our fantasies. And no one nourishes it more assiduously than our children's authors. And that is why, if I was asked, I would cast my vote for Enid Blyton's dreamy bike trips, where the adults fade quickly into the background, over S.E. Hinton's gritty tales. I cast my vote for the island where there are no adults; and for sleeping in the woods, and walking the shoreline to Brighton, and for all the eight-year-old waitresses, wherever they are.

1 May 2005

FREE BOOKS

I was walking through my neighbourhood when I came across a cardboard box full of books. The box was half on the sidewalk and half on the front lawn of whomever they belonged to. It was clear whoever that was was finished with the books and had put them out so that people who came along and felt like going through them were welcome both to do that and to take away whatever books struck their fancy.

It is a conspicuous and uncomfortable business going through someone else's garbage but not as uncomfortable a business as walking by a box full of free books. I looked around, and when I saw no one was watching, I knelt down and tried to flip through the box as fast I could. I was hoping that I could get the job done before the owner walked out of his house and spotted me. I know I was doing what he intended me to do, but I found the possibility of him watching me embarrassing.

So, there I was, on my knees, going through the box, when it became apparent that I had stumbled upon a treasure trove. Not that these books had any great value, just that whoever it was who had chucked them out had been living my life.

What was there? Well, to start with, there was *Gateway to Latin,* 101 pages of pain that I carried with me, or, more to the point, didn't carry with me, all the way through grade ten. There was *Man and His World,* a reader that begins with the eloquent address delivered by William Faulkner in 1950 when he received the Nobel Prize for literature, and there was *Contemporary English One.*

There was popular literature as well. *Love Story* by Eric Segal, for example, which I reread standing there on the pavement: "What can you say about a twenty-five-year-old girl who died? That she was beautiful. And brilliant. That she loved Mozart, and Bach. And the Beatles. And me."

I stuffed *Love Story* into my pocket for old time's sake, and it was just after I did that I found the real treasure. A book that I'm sure you've never heard of, but a book that swept me away when I read it in 1969: *The Strawberry Statement: Notes of a College Revolutionary* by James Simon Kunen.

I hadn't seen *The Strawberry Statement* since I was gliding up and down the escalators of Sir George Williams University in my beige corduroy jacket.

I was so transported to have the book in my hands again that I didn't notice the kid come out of the house until he was halfway down the walk. He looked at me the way you might look at someone going through your garbage.

I was beyond caring.

"These your dad's?" I asked.

"Yeah," said the kid. "We're cleaning out the attic."

"Your dad," I said, hefting Kunen's book, "he's about fifty-two years old, right?"

"Exactly," said the kid, slowing down and looking at me for the first time. "How'd you know that?"

"Just a hunch," I said.

He left for school, I guess. I finished pawing through the box. I pocketed *The Strawberry Statement* and, like I already said, *Love Story,* and the two readers, and the Latin text.

Five old books, but they were once part of my life, and it felt good running into them like that, unexpectedly, on a cloudy morning in November. Like running into a group of old friends. I brought them to my office. They are there today, on my desk. Sometimes you can get as much pleasure looking at a book as you can from reading it. So they are going to stay where I can see them, until I get tired of them. Then, who knows, maybe I'll put them into a box of my own on my lawn and see who I reel in.

19 November 2000

THE CREATION
OF SAM McGEE

There have been, over the years, many attempts to get down on paper the essence of a Canadian winter. I think of the opening paragraphs of Hugh MacLennan's quintessential Canadian novel *Two Solitudes* and his poetic description of Montreal's Sherbrooke Street on a snowy winter night. I think of William Kurelek's sunny prairie paintings, of David Blackwood's dark etchings of the great Newfoundland sealing disaster of 1914.

They all get part of it; they all come close to it in their own way, but none of them get closer to the heart of the matter, closer to the bone-numbing chill of a January wind, than Robert W. Service, the bard of the Yukon, gets in that most famous of his poems, "The Cremation of Sam McGee."

You know how it goes:

There are strange things done in the midnight sun
By the men who moil for gold;
The Arctic trails have their secret tales
That would make your blood run cold;
The Northern Lights have seen queer sights,
But the queerest they ever did see

Was that night on the marge of Lake Lebarge
I cremated Sam McGee.

Now that is what I call poetry—an epic *chiller* about the night Sam McGee froze to death on the Klondike Trail and then sprung back to life, for a moment, on his funeral pyre.

It begins thus:

Now Sam McGee was from Tennessee
Where the cotton blooms and blows ...

Well, guess what? That's not even close to being true. Not at all. Sam McGee was actually from Peterborough, Ontario. Well, Lindsay, to be precise.

I know this. I have been to his grave. I have spoken to a number of his descendants. I have met his granddaughter.

William Sam McGee. Born in 1867 of Irish parents, he was a prospector—a sourdough. He had a bank account at the Canadian Bank of Commerce in Dawson City where young Robert Service worked as a teller.

Many of Service's readers assume that the poet was a hard-boiled, long-gone Klondike prospector himself. He was a bank teller. And he lived until 1958. He saw McGee's name on the bank ledger and pilfered it for his poem. Without permission, it seems.

Sam McGee might have moiled for gold, but he didn't expire in a snowstorm on the edge of Lake Lebarge. He died of a stroke, I believe it was, on his daughter's farm not far from Calgary. I thought it was high time someone set the record straight.

If you would permit me then: "The Creation of Sam McGee,

the sequel." The poem Service would surely have written had he made it to *Sequelsville*. I include it here with a nod to this long winter, and deep apologies to all concerned.

There are strange things done 'neath the midnight sun
By bank tellers who work in the cold.
The arctic banks have their secret ranks
Of writers and poets I'm told.
The Northern Lights have seen queer sights,
But the queerest they ever did see
Was the night on the marge of Lake Lebarge
I created Sam McGee.

Now Sam McGee weren't from Tennessee; that was just a
writer's trick.
And when I think today of what he had to say, of my poem
it makes me sick.
I took his name, if it's all the same, from a list on my desk
at the bank.
It's what writers do, when they're brewing a stew, to stop it
from getting too rank.

He came in one day, and I said, "Hey, I hope you don't
mind what I wrote."
And he turned to me and, "Bob," says he as he reached
out and grabbed at my throat.
"It's been thirty long years, and we have some arrears, to
settle between us two.
So listen up well, 'cause my life has been hell, and I'm
feeling mighty blue.

"I'm from Lindsay, you see, not from Tennessee, and I'm
   still living, I guess you could say.
I lit out from home when I was barely a gnome, fifteen
   years if I was a day.
I've been travelling around, but I've come back to town,
   'cause I'm feeling so poorly and lame.
And I see by the door at the old general store they're
   selling my last remains."

He plunked a jug down and I stared with a frown as the
   ashes spilled out on my desk.
And he let my throat go and said, "I want you to know I've
   come to you with my dying request."
He seemed so low that I couldn't say no, then he began
   with a moaning sound
and said, "When I'm gone and it's time to move on, I want
   to be put in the ground."

Well, a man's last need is a thing to heed, so I swore I
   would not fail.
He said, "It's the fear of the fire drawing near that is
   making my skin so pale."
I said, "It's just a poem that I wrote coming home from a
   party a long time ago."
And he said through the tears of thirty long years, "You
   doomed me to burn when I go."

He crouched by my desk and raved for the rest of the night
  of his fear of the fire.
I said, "Those ashes you bought, it's a tourist shop, don't
  make a small thing so dire.
You ain't yet dead," I said, shaking my head, but he
  laughed and he started to glow.
"It's the fevers," he said. "Get me a bed. I want clean
  sheets when I go."

For a day and a night he kept up the fight as he sweated
  his life away.
A fever so hot that, believe it or not, he singed the sheets
  the next day.
And at dawn on the third, I give you my word, all that was
  left to see
Was a small pile of dust, and I knew it was just, what
  remained of Sam McGee.

There are strange things done 'neath the midnight sun
By bank tellers who work in the cold.
The arctic banks have their secret ranks
Of writers and poets I'm told.
The Northern Lights have seen queer sights,
But the queerest they ever did see
Was the night on the marge of Lake Lebarge
I created Sam McGee.

18 January 2009

QUENTIN REYNOLDS

A bookshelf is a highly personal thing, and often the books on it bristle with emotional connections that no one would ever guess. There are the old friends that you put on the shelf and return to often, acquaintances that sit there for years, untouched; there are the ones that slip away and are forgotten, and those that seem to wander off on their own accord, yet remain, ghostlike, to haunt the library, like an old lover, with feelings of regret, or sorrow, or confusion. These are the books you think of from time to time and wonder what became of them, and if you would have anything to say to one another if you were in touch again.

I have such a book. It was written by the American war journalist Quentin Reynolds. It was called *By Quentin Reynolds*. I owned it in a pocketbook, and it made a big impression. Reynolds, as I recall, seemed to be on a first-name basis with Winston Churchill and just about anyone else who you would want to be on first-name basis with in the 1940s.

Probably that book had something to do with me doing what I do, and have done, on the radio these past twenty-five odd years.

I don't remember how it came into my possession;

probably I stumbled on it in the drugstore, which is where I used to buy my books. In any case, it made an impression— it was one of those books you read when you are a kid that expands your understanding of the world, mainly because it is full of stuff you had no idea existed.

So it was a deal for me, and like a fool, one day, I sold it. I did this on a spring afternoon when I was supposed to be studying for exams. I wanted to go to a movie, and I didn't have any money, so I boxed up my entire book collection and took the box to a second-hand bookstore and sold everything— including that formative Quentin Reynolds autobiography.

I spent the next four or five years regretting that, until the day I found myself, by chance, walking past the second-hand bookstore where I had done the deed. I wandered in and began looking through the stacks of books while a sort of melancholy settled over me, when low and behold, I came across the book I had sold, the very copy. I plucked it out of the pile and saw my name written in the inside.

I bought it back of course, for three times the price I had sold it for; storage fees, I guess. I held on to it for a long time, and then, somewhere over the years, I lost track of it again.

I have no idea what brought it back to mind, or what I would make of it if I got my hands on a copy today. I am not at all sure how Quentin Reynolds would strike me now that he and I have walked down the same road a little ways. One never knows with old friends. Sometimes reunions can be deep and joyful things. Other times there are nothing but awkward silences and promises to call that are never kept.

20 November 2005

LEACOCK COUNTRY

The little village of Sutton, Ontario, recently swallowed by the town of Georgina, sticks to the south shore of Lake Simcoe like an old photo in a family album.

Walking along the Hedge Road in Sutton, an evocatively narrow and twisty road that runs right along the edge of the lake, it is easy to pretend, as I often do when I walk along it, that you are strolling through the British countryside. That is how I was preoccupying myself the other day when I happened upon Canadian broadcaster Peter Gzowski's old cottage, where I spent so many happy New Year's Eves, and which, I feel compelled to report, has been painted an arresting shade of mauve since Peter sold it. Someone has also cut down Gzowski's favourite (and don't think the old tobacco bum wouldn't appreciate the irony) Smoke Tree.

I wasn't in Sutton, however, to inspect or pass judgment on Gzowski's old cottage; time marches wearily on, and so did I, along the Hedge Road, past The Briars, past Gzowski's and over the one-lane-only, historically designated 1912 iron bridge that spans the Black River.

I was heading to Peter Sibbald Brown's house and studio, to visit the man who famously plucked a burning log off the living-room floor one smoky afternoon long ago, and whose wit and charm had saved the day for Gzowksi so many other times over the years.

I was going to see PSB, as Gzowski affectionately dubbed him, partly because there are few people in this world who can make me laugh quite as joyfully as he does, and mostly because I had, over lunch that day, learned that Peter Sibbald Brown, who is a collector and an award-winning and elegant designer of books, happened to be working with six or seven handwritten original pages of Stephen Leacock's manuscript from *Sunshine Sketches of a Little Town.*

Leacock, as you no doubt know, is Canada's answer to Mark Twain. He was the most famous humorist *in the world* in the early days of the twentieth century. In fact, it has been famously said that in his prime, more people had heard of Leacock than had heard of Canada.

Sunshine Sketches is Leacock's enduring Canadian master-piece. It was published in 1912, almost one hundred years ago and still sells several thousand copies a year in the New Canadian Library edition.

So I made my way over the bridge and past the little church where Leacock is buried, for this is Leacock country. He grew up and summered on the shores of Lake Simcoe. He knew all the little towns around and about.

When I finally got to PSB's house, I found the manuscript on his work table—an unlined piece of brown paper that I reached out to touch in awe. As far as Canadian letters are concerned, the piece of paper that was lying in front of me is just about the fountainhead.

Leacock, it turns out, wrote with a straight pen. You can see, right on the page, the various spots where the ink is fainter, the exact places where he had run out. You can tell, when it darkens, the moment he had paused and dipped his pen into the inkwell. Although it didn't look like there was a lot of pausing going on.

"Yes," said PSB, smiling, "it looks like he was really galloping along, doesn't it?" PSB had studied the *entire* manuscript. "There are very few revisions, anywhere," he said.

We stood there, marvelling over the single page for a good thirty minutes, trying our best to wring some meaning out of it. And then I headed back to my hotel room, in some sort of dreamy state, feeling both connected and wistful about the past. What would I ask Leacock, I wondered, if he was alive today? What would I want to tell him?

When I finally got to my room, I pulled out the copy of *Sunshine Sketches* that I had brought with me, and I spent the rest of that evening dipping into the sardonic elegance of Leacock's prose.

From Chapter Three: "The Marine Excursion of the Knights of Pythias," a story from *Sunshine Sketches* that recounts the "sinking" of the paddle wheeler *The Mariposa Belle*. I place "sinking" in quotations because, well, I'm not going to recount the whole episode wherein the sinking ship ends up floating, and then rescuing, the sinking rescue boats. But consider this lovely moment when the townsfolk from Mariposa are climbing aboard the *Mariposa Belle,* before the excursion begins, which Leacock has explained will be totally dry, except of course for the two kegs of beer, which don't count, because the Knights of Pythias are, of course, by their very constitution dedicated to temperance.

"And there's Henry Mullins, the manager of the Exchange Bank, ... with a small flask of Pogram's Special in his hip pocket as a sort of ..." and here is Leacock's brilliant flourish, "a sort of amendment to the constitution."

That is why people still want to read Leacock.

Mind you, many of the citizens of Orillia who felt they were being lampooned when the book arrived didn't. But they just didn't get it. Didn't understand that affection and kindness were the cornerstones of Leacock's house of humour. His eye was focused through the sardonic lens of *irony*—not sarcasm or satire. And when he wrote of the town of Sutton, where I am staying this week, that it was "an orderly little place, dull as ditchwater, but quite unaware of the fact," you have to remember he chose to be buried in Sutton, and appreciate that the telling phrase isn't that it was dull but that it had the redeeming quality of being unaware of the fact.

Leacock, who could sound disparaging, believed deeply that humour should be, more than anything, *kind*, that one should laugh *with,* and not *at,* others.

The provincial in me would like to think that this was his Canadian upbringing revealing itself, but if I were honest, I would have to acknowledge it's what you see in the best of Twain, whom Leacock admired so much.

And, if you're so inclined, you can follow the thread of kindness as it weaves together all the great American and Canadian humorists who have written since. Or the ones I think are great anyway.

My hero, E.B. White, for one, who as well as *Charlotte's Web* wrote many humorous pieces for *The New Yorker* magazine and then, achingly, warned that you should *avoid* humour if you are concerned for your reputation as a writer. The world *likes* humour, wrote White, but treats it patronizingly, decorating its serious artists with laurels and its wags with Brussels sprouts. Writers who take their literary selves with great seriousness, says White in his essay "On Humor," are at considerable pains never to associate their names with anything funny.

And yet, and yet.

No less a serious person than that cagey old constitutional expert Senator Eugene Forsey said of Stephen Leacock, who held a Ph.D. from the University of Chicago, that he could have been anything he wanted, including prime minister of Canada. And Leacock? Leacock, who had an abiding interest in politics, said he would rather have written *Alice in Wonderland* than the entire *Encyclopaedia Britannica*.

And even poor old E.B. White, who mostly wrote kind and funny, and never thought of himself as a success because of it, knew that there is a fine line between laughing and crying. And when it is done right, that a piece of humorous writing can bring a person to the point where his or her emotional responses are untrustworthy, to that place where tears and laughter meet. Humour can do that, wrote White, because it plays close to the big hot fire that is truth. Sometimes the reader feels the heat.

I stayed up much later than I expected that night looking for the heat in Leacock, finding plenty.

And thinking of E.B. White, whom I admire so much, I remembered Mordecai Richler, who allowed me to audit his class at Sir George Williams University one winter long ago, and W.O. Mitchell, who befriended me when I was beginning to write, and showed me, by his own joyful example, that it is permissible to rejoice in one's own work when you read it out loud. (Leacock, I am told, didn't work out on CBC Radio because of his habit of chuckling at his own jokes before delivering them.)

Mitchell, White and Richler were all Leacock's children in a way, and all of them are gone now.

Finally I went to sleep, with the sort of melancholy that can only come with a really funny story.

PSB woke me the next morning.

"I forgot to tell you the most astonishing thing," he said over the phone. "When Henry Fox Talbot was inventing photography, he didn't call it photography. And pictures weren't called photographs. You know what he called them? He was using the natural light of the sun. He called them 'sunshine sketches.' Isn't that astonishing?"

So that is what Leacock was up to, and Twain before him, and Richler and Mitchell and the rest who have come and gone since.

Taking pictures.

"I throw ink at the wolf to keep it from the door," wrote Leacock once, in a letter, trying to explain his job as a writer.

The thing about him was he kept hitting the wolf. But softly, and with affectionate and kind contemplation on the incongruities of life. God bless him. We were lucky he passed our way. Lucky still, because mercifully whenever we want, we can, with the flip of a page and God's good grace, still feel his heat.

23 March 2008

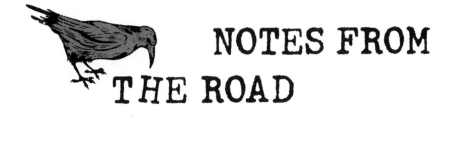

NOTES FROM
THE ROAD

THE WAY WHICH
IS NOT THE WAY

We set off from Sault Ste. Marie, heading for Timmins. Our bus driver, John, had the route carefully worked out. The impulse, when you're moving from town to town with a bus full of performers and assorted technicians, is to get where you're going as fast as you can.

"We'll go up Highway 17," said John. "We'll cut off at Wawa. It won't take us more than six hours."

Everyone settled into their seats. And everything was going fine. Until *I* got a hold of the map.

"Hey," I said, "look at this. If we turn onto Highway 556, we'll save over a hundred kilometres."

Before I go further, you should know this about me: if we were in a car together, you and I, and you were driving, and we came to one of those moments where you pulled over and looked at me uncertainly, and said, "I'm not sure, what do you think? Left? Or right?" I would, reflexively and consistently, choose the back road. Fast roads bore me. I like it when roads are winding and narrow, and there are places you can stop that don't feel like the place where you stopped two hours ago. I like the slow way. On the question of shortcuts, were you to call it to a question, I would vote with both feet. You can mark me down in favour.

I say this because it has been my experience that shortcuts are hardly ever shorter. In fact, it has been my experience that shortcuts are almost certainly *longer*. If a *clock* is something you pay attention to, that is. If *timing* your way through life is something you do. If you believe that by getting there faster, you get *more* time.

The thing about shortcuts is that they are just called *short* so people like me can convince others to give them a go. "Come *on*," we say. "It's a *short*cut." The unspoken lie, of course, is the implication that it'll be faster than the other way, the longer way around, that we are saving time here; in fact, we might be *gaining time*.

If we were to tell the truth, if we were to say, "It's a *long*cut. If we go my way, it will take longer, and we could get hopelessly lost, and maybe there will be bears," well, who would follow us then?

The sign at the beginning of Highway 556 was our first clue: *No gas for the next 86 kilometres*.

John had pulled the bus onto the shoulder. We were weighing our options.

"Don't worry," I said. "It'll be fine. John filled the gas tank at breakfast. Right?"

And so we set off. Ten minutes later, when the road turned from a double-lane highway to a gravel logging road, bass player Dennis Pendrith put down his *Rolling Stone* magazine and began staring out the bus window. Before long Dennis had his face pressed to the window the way people stare out of small planes when they are landing in a snowstorm.

Suddenly John slammed his foot on the air brakes of our big tour bus and we came to a shuddering stop.

"What's happening?" I asked cheerfully from my seat near the back.

"Oh," said Dennis gloomily, "nothing really."

Dennis still had his faced pressed to the window.

"Unless," added John, the driver, "you call a bear in the middle of the road something."

Pretty soon everyone was gathered at the front window of our bus, huddled around it like kids watching a video at a birthday party.

No one moved as we bounced past Vixen Lake. No one moved as we skirted Gordon Lake. And no one moved at the end of Ranger Lake as we crept over a wooden bridge barely wide enough for a bus.

We only encountered one other vehicle on that road, a logging truck, heading in the opposite direction. I can't imagine what he thought when our forty-five-foot tour bus pulled onto the shoulder to let him pass.

We eventually rolled into Timmins, safe and sound. Although, admittedly, a lot later than we would have if we hadn't taken my shortcut. But that's the way it is with shortcuts—turn right to avoid a traffic jam, and three hours later you're sitting in someone's kitchen talking to them about the problems they're having with their milk cows. Crazy things happen when you take the way which is not the way. Sometimes, the craziest of all, they're even faster. But that doesn't happen often.

20 November 2005

IN PRAISE
OF CURLING

The Vinyl Cafe producer Jess Milton was behind the wheel. I was sitting beside her, my feet on the dash, a map in my lap. We were heading west along the Trans-Canada Highway. We had left Winnipeg after breakfast, and now were coming up on Portage la Prairie, where we were meant to cut off onto the Yellowhead. We made the turn and continued northwest, past all the little railway towns: Woodside, Gladstone and Neepawa. We arrived in Minnedosa in the afternoon and got a hotel room, and dinner, and directions to the hamlet of Clanwilliam, which we had been told might be the best place in the country to spend some time if we wanted to learn a few things about curling.

Clanwilliam is ten kilometres north of Minnedosa, but getting there can be confusing the first time you try, and we made a couple of false starts.

When we did get there, we stopped, as we had been instructed, at the general store to ask directions. We were looking for the Clanwilliam curling rink. But if the general store was the only place we saw in Clanwilliam, we wouldn't have gone home unhappy. The general store would have been worth the trip.

The Clanwilliam general store is perfect in every way. It has wooden floors and a wood-burning stove. It has groceries, and it has penny candy, but not too much of either. It has a kitchen table where folks gather in the morning to have coffee. And a pool table—a buck a game. And in an alcove at the very back, behind the wood stove and the kitchen table and the pool table, a single old-time barber chair, empty the evening we stopped by, but there for the itinerant barber who comes to town every second Thursday. Haircuts, $10.

We were worried the store might not be open. We had heard what had happened the last time a reporter had been sent to Clanwilliam to visit the Clanwilliam Curling Club. It was a sports reporter from the *Boston Globe*. Like us, he had been told to stop in at the general store for directions to the rink. When he got there, all he found was a sign in the store window that read, *GONE CURLING*.

Not that finding the rink should have been difficult. Clanwilliam is really no more than a crossroads. There are only about forty souls living in Clanwilliam today. Besides the general store and the curling rink, Clanwilliam has a grain elevator, a community hall and a repair shop. Not much, but an impressive list of facilities for a town of forty. If you offered services like that for every forty people in the city where I live, you would have to erect a community centre and a curling club on every city block.

Happily the general store *was* open when we arrived, and we went in, bought some penny candy and got directions.

It turns out we were only a block away. We drove around the corner, parked beside everyone else in the shadow of the grain elevator and walked through the snow toward a long, narrow Quonset hut that looked like a cross between a bowling alley and a garage.

There was an outdoor skating rink beside the door, with two battered hockey nets at either end. It was half the size of an official rink, but plenty big enough for a game of shinny.

We stood there for a moment under a bone-white moon and looked at each other. We didn't have to say what we were thinking. It was a perfect prairie moment. Our horizon was framed by a grain elevator, an outdoor skating rink and the door to a natural-ice curling arena. Neither of us knew anything about curling, but now we knew why we had been sent to Clanwilliam to learn about it.

I opened the door. We stepped into what might have been someone's basement rec room. The end of the Quonset was covered in wood panelling. There was a coat rack to our left and above it twelve pairs of skates lined up on a shelf.

"Oh," said Jim Richards, who was the first person we met, "that's where everyone leaves their skates. If you want to go skating, feel free to borrow a pair."

There was a small kitchen in the far corner, serving homemade hamburgers and lemon meringue pie; a large table in the other one with a cribbage board; and two rows of twelve chairs overlooking the ice surface. The chairs were salvaged from the Ericson Theatre when it closed.

We stayed for three hours. We sat in the seats and watched the rocks lumbering along the ice surface from one end of the rink to the other, smashing into one another with prehistoric booms. Curling, a game invented in Scotland's hinterland, seems to have been made for the granite grip of a Canadian winter.

"You gotta have some pie," said twenty-year-old Andrew Richards.

"Why?" we asked

"Best pie in the world," said Andrew.

We ate pie and burgers. But most importantly, we fell in love with curling.

When we left, we were of the opinion that curling may just be the perfect Canadian game, and we were berating ourselves for wasting so many of our winters.

Where should I begin? Maybe where every curler I met always begins. With fellowship.

Curling is a sport that fosters fellowship. That is easy to say. And lots of people would say it about their sport. The thing is, curlers mean it. Curlers seem a little closer to each other than others. Every game begins and ends with a handshake. It's tradition. And curlers don't mess with tradition. The game unfolds slowly. It allows conversation, not only among team members but between teams. You spend a lot of time standing on the ice, leaning on your broom beside the other curler, and eventually you have to say something.

Bad shots are ignored, good shots are complimented.

And when the handshakes are over, the fellowship isn't. There is another tradition. The winning team buys the losing team a drink. In the old days before liquor licences, you went down to the basement, to the "snake pit," for your drink. These days you go to the bar. And even if you are playing in a big bonspiel and have an early game the next day, even if you are tired and need to go to sleep, you stay and talk. You linger. You get to know the people you play with and against. You replay the good shots and argue about the strategies. Sometimes it is hard to tell where the game begins and ends.

It is a surprisingly physical game, hard on the knees. You have to be in good shape if you are really sweeping hard. Two curlers who can really sweep can move a stone an extra ten to fifteen feet, so a skip with two good sweeps can throw to them, and they can take the rock home.

You can, nevertheless, play at any age. We saw an eighty-four-year-old, whose knees can no longer take the strain, using a special cane to push her rocks down the ice.

"Oh," said Jim. "You see that a lot these days. No one minds. It helps people play longer."

Name me another sport so forgiving to seniors.

And while we're on the topic of seniors, I have heard some people say curling is boring. I say you give a team of seniors a bunch of forty-two-pound rocks and tell them to run up and down a sheet of ice, and I think you have an arena full of excitement.

But it wasn't just seniors we saw playing in Clanwilliam. We met a seven-year-old who had been curling for two years. He was there with his grandfather, his uncle and his cousin. We saw a mom and dad playing on the same team with their teenage kids. This is a sport that is designed for families and neighbours. All you need is four people for a team.

And it's cheap. An annual membership at the Clanwilliam Curling Club costs $20. Unless you're a student. Then it's $15. The club provides the rocks. All you need is a broom and a pair of shoes.

Everything at the Clanwilliam Curling Club is affordable. Pie? A dollar. Pop? A dollar. Coffee? A dollar for as much as you can drink in a night. The whole thing is run on the honour system. Just like the game.

There are no refs in curling. You call your own penalties. If your broom touches your rock, or burns it, as they say, you're expected to remove the rock from the game. Nine times out of ten you could get away with the infraction. No one tries.

Okay, there *are* umpires at the big bonspiels, but they are kept behind glass. And they don't interfere unless they're asked. It is a gentleman's game. I don't know how you say that inclusively. And I don't want to insult all the women who play just as ... gentlemanly, on teams with other women and, I should point out, on teams with men. But I don't think I have to fuss about that: curlers don't take offence easily.

I have a friend back home, a young mother who plays at the provincial level. I phoned after my visit to Clanwilliam.

"What do *you* like about the game?" I asked.

Like every curler I spoke with, she talked about fellowship.

"But besides that," I said.

"Well, you get to yell," she said.

"Yell?" I said.

"Sure," she said. "Who doesn't like to yell? Especially curling talk. HURRY HARD," she yelled down the phone line. "Hurry hard. Now how great is it to yell *that* in public?"

So, yes, I'm loving this sport, though I may be getting ahead of myself. I haven't actually played. But maybe that is the best place to keep your favourite sport, at arm's length, in the realm where anything is possible. I still have a lot to learn, for instance, how to read the scoreboard. As far as I can figure, some drunk in a kilt developed the system years ago and people have been trying to make sense of it ever since.

"It's just the way we do it," is the best explanation I got.

Mostly, I think, I have fallen for curling because, more than any other sport I know, it is about community. And, I would put forward, sport is at its best the closer it can get to that. Take hockey, for instance. Professional hockey was at its best when it reflected the community it came from. Bruce Kidd and John Macfarlane have written about this eloquently. In the 1950s, Rocket Richard and the Montreal Canadiens more than *personified* Montreal. They *were* Montreal. The team might have underpaid Richard, but they *never* would have traded him. The community would not have accepted that. Today, professional athletes are only seldom connected to the communities where they play. They are *literally* free agents. They pop up wherever it suits them.

The best of hockey was never the professional game. The best was when the old senior leagues from coast to coast competed each year for the Allen Cup and the right to represent Canada in the World Championship. In those days any community could dream of sending their team overseas.

That is why, when I grew up in Montreal, I grew up wondering about towns like Trail, British Columbia, and Whitby, Ontario—homes to the Trail Smokeaters and the Whitby Dunlops. And why, when I was a man, and I found myself in Trail, the first thing I did was visit the hockey arena.

Well, curling still works like that. The Briars (for men) and Scotties Tournament of Hearts (for women) are the top rungs for Canadian curlers.

And when the curling season begins each year, every curler in the country begins the season in the knowledge that they *could* make it to either tournament. Anyone in any town, in any province, has the same shot.

And this is not just in theory. This is the way it works. Club playoffs, in every club in the country, are played to choose the teams that will go to the zone playoffs; which are played to determine which teams go to provincial playoffs; which are played to determine the twelve provincial and territorial champions that go to the Briars and the Tournament of Hearts.

You have to love a sport where any schmo can aspire to playing at a national level. It is, ultimately, a sport of the people.

2 February 2009

ROBERT STANFIELD'S GRAVE

I have an affection for graveyards. And when I found myself in Halifax, Nova Scotia, with time on my hands, I decided to go for a walk in one. I considered the Old Burying Ground, on the corner of Barrington and Spring Garden. The Old Burying Ground is Halifax's first graveyard, established in 1749, and it looks like something Charles Dickens might have imagined. I might also have chosen Mount Olivet, Baron de Hirsch or Fairview and paid my respects to the one hundred and fifty victims from the sinking of the *Titanic* who are buried there. I *almost* did that, as I seem to remember having read that *Titanic* director James Cameron took the name for Leonardo DiCaprio's character from an actual Halifax tomb, and that there were always fresh flowers on that grave, and many visitors. I thought that might be a worthwhile distraction, but, while I was trying to verify that, I learned Robert Stanfield was buried in Camp Hill, across the street from the Halifax Public Gardens, which more or less means in the centre of town, and I decided to pay my respects to him instead.

Stanfield, sadly, might need an introduction these days, and the best one I can give is that after he served four terms as the premier of Nova Scotia, he was elected leader of the

Progressive Conservative Party of Canada. This was back in the 1960s, when the word *progressive* meant something. His nickname, which he came by honestly, was Honest Bob. There are plenty of people still standing who would tell you Bob Stanfield was the best prime minister Canada never had.

I once spent an afternoon with Bob Stanfield. It was during his retirement, and we sat and talked in his backyard garden. What I remember most fondly about our time together was the moment I asked him to show me his favourite part of the garden.

"That would depend," he replied, "on the time of day."

He went on to explain how his appreciation of the garden shifted with the sun. Bob Stanfield was a modest man who understood the beauty of light through leaves. I liked him, and I can't for the life of me remember if I voted for him. Once, I think.

So as I set off, I felt I was visiting an old friend of sorts.

The sign on the cemetery's iron gate read, *Open at Dawn, closed at Dusk,* which struck me as all the precision anyone would want on a graveyard sign. Like at many cemeteries, there is a ring road at Camp Hill and then two roads that bisect the graveyard into four quadrants. In the exact centre, where the roads meet, I found an abandoned white chapel. There was a phone number posted for information.

I called the number and told the man who answered that I wanted to see Stanfield's grave.

There was a slight pause, and he explained that while he was happy to give me directions to Stanfield's grave, and he did do that, he didn't think I would find it.

"There is no stone," he said. "It was removed. His third wife is fighting about it with his children."

I didn't ask what they were fighting about and considered for a moment calling his children to find out, but I decided the twice-widowed Stanfield deserved the privacy and respect in death that he would have granted others in life. The family would settle things soon enough, and he would get his stone back.

Undoubtedly both sides were acting out of their own sense of love and loyalty. And sadness, of course.

I sat on one of the benches for a while with a sense of something that felt like sadness myself, which is not at all what I had come there for, and then I decided that there would be another stone that would have something to say to me if I gave it a chance, so I set off to see if I could find it.

A graveyard can be many things: a park, a garden, a museum, a history lesson, a conversation with the past. The nice thing about *walking* in one is that people are usually on their best behaviour. They don't tend to litter, or panhandle, or do anything too offensive in graveyards, and if you *should* come upon someone on one of the footpaths, they usually give you wide berth or, at most, a solemn nod, in case, I suppose, you are there on some sad mission.

Even the dead, on the whole, are at their best. All in all, the monuments are modest. There is not a lot of bad taste in a graveyard.

Camp Hill is indeed tasteful, if agreeably cockeyed. Stones tipping higgledy-piggledy like crooked teeth. There is a semblance of order, with orchardlike rows to walk down, but it is the order of an old orchard, slightly messy and, you sense, verging on out of control.

Like all graveyards, or most anyway, it is overwhelmingly green: all leaves, and grass, and on the oldest tombs emerald-coloured moss, made all the more lovely by the white and grey stone.

The nice thing about Camp Hill is that no one seems in a hurry to fix things. The stones have been left as they fall or lean, which might be upsetting if it's your grandmother's stone that has fallen, but all together it gives you the feeling of wandering through an ancient forest; the deadfalls are part of the beauty.

There is a sign at the gate, which I missed on the way in but will catch on the way out, that says, *Warning. Gravestones and monuments may fall over and cause injury.* Which, I suppose, is technically true, but I imagine you would have to be pretty lucky to be there when a stone falls and exceptionally *unlucky* to be under it when it happens.

But then I am reminded that bad luck *does* happen, as it did to Gerald Keeping, age eight, and Bernard Johnson, age ten, *buried together,* reads their joint inscription.

As they lived so they rest, killed, I read on their shared stone, *by auto in the spring of 1931.*

Sometime after that, as I wandered up and down the rows, I came upon Sir William Young's grave. Sir William was born in Scotland in 1799 and was, I learn, once the chief justice of Nova Scotia, *a brilliant orator, an eminent lawyer and a distinguished statesman, whose gifts and bequeaths to charitable and educational institutions in Halifax mark his high estimate* and these are the words that catch my eye, *mark his high estimate of the duties and privileges of citizenship.*

The duties and privileges of citizenship are not the duties and privileges we mull often these days. It is good to be reminded of them.

I was in Wales last summer, and one afternoon I went for a walk. Walking through that green land, I felt the closest I ever have felt to being in heaven—there were rolling hills and green fields and sheep grazing in pastures, the hedgerows had little steps so you could step over them, and in the distance there was a village that I imagined had little pubs where you could have a pint if you were thirsty when you got there. Walking in the Camp Hill Cemetery reminded me of my walk in Wales, although it didn't feel nearly as close to heaven. It was too contained and, strangely, too old, and Robert Stanfield doesn't have a tombstone. But it was green, and no one bothered me, and the wind was in the trees. Just as I was about to take my leave, the sun came out, through the leaves, and the quality of the light changed. I thought about Stanfield again, and that afternoon in his garden, and how the light through the leaves would have pleased him. And it might not have been heaven, but it was close enough for a Monday afternoon.

8 July 2007

THE IMPERIAL THEATRE, SAINT JOHN, NEW BRUNSWICK

One morning as I sat in my hotel room in Saint John, New Brunswick, just back from the Saint John City Market, where I had bought a supply of the oily smoked salmon you can get there, I received a phone call from a man I didn't know. He wanted to tell me a story and was wondering if we could meet. His friend, who had passed away the week before, had been instrumental in the restoration of the Imperial Theatre—the theatre where I would be performing that evening. The man on the phone was hoping, by way of tribute, that I might mention his friend at my show. I would, after all, be playing on the stage that she had been so involved in saving.

The Imperial, a grand, soft-seater from the vaudeville era, happens to be one of my favourite theatres in Canada. I didn't, however, know much about it. I had read that it had opened in 1913 and had welcomed some of the biggest theatrical names of that era, including Ethel Barrymore, John Phillip Sousa and Harry Houdini. And I knew it had eventually fallen into disrepair and then had been lovingly restored with gold gilt, a huge chandelier and deep red wallpaper: "the most beautifully restored theatre in Canada," wrote *The Globe and*

Mail. It was the story of the restoration the man wanted me to hear. I agreed to meet him.

In 1929, Jack MacDougall told me, the grand old Imperial had become a movie theatre. It remained so for almost three decades. And then came television, and the Imperial, like so many other theatres of its kind, closed its doors. It was bought by a church group—the Full Gospel Assembly—who renovated it and used it as a church until Jack's friend, the schoolteacher Susan Bate, walked into the story. That was in the early 1980s.

"It was the summertime," said Jack.

"I noticed a small ad in a local paper, that the Full Gospel Assembly was offering, at auction, the theatre organ. I told Susan. It made her crazy. She made me run home and get the paper so she could see the ad for herself.

"When she saw it, she said, 'We can't let this happen. We can't let them sell off New Brunswick's heritage as if it doesn't matter.'"

Jack MacDougall was an unemployed taxi driver that summer. And that day, he happened to have his mind on a date. It wasn't to happen. Susan Bate was so exorcised by the ad that she badgered him into cancelling the date.

"This is your responsibility," she told him. "You saw the ad."

The sale was to take place the next morning at nine o'clock.

MacDougall and Bate spent the rest of that night at Reggie's Restaurant organizing a committee. The next morning MacDougall, who was the only one without a job, was dispatched to the sale. It turned out he was the only one who showed up.

The lady from the church said, "Wait here," and she began turning on the church lights one by one.

"I'll never forget it," said Jack. "It was a vision of beauty. The church was a theatre. A theatre I didn't know existed."

The organ, a Wurlitzer, was in a thousand pieces. MacDougall was more interested in the building. He was enthralled by it.

He arranged to meet the board of the church. They thought he was coming to talk to them about the organ.

"I wasn't sure why I asked to see them," he said. "I was in a bit of a fog. And then halfway through the meeting I just blurted it out. I asked them if they would be interested in selling me the theatre."

They laughed.

"We wouldn't sell this theatre for a million dollars."

And that was when MacDougall said, "A million dollars seems like a fair price to me."

He offered them a dollar as a down payment. They threw him out.

But as luck would have it, the board had a constitutional obligation to take any offer of sale to the congregation. The following week the pastor announced that an unemployed taxi driver had offered to buy their church for a million dollars.

The congregation erupted. No one wanted the building sold. It was, after all, the place where many of them had been baptised and married, and where they had said goodbye to their beloved deceased.

More to get the meeting under the control than anything, the pastor suggested they seek a sign from God. They would pass the following Saturday in fast and prayer and seek God's direction.

That Friday, Jack MacDougall went to the pastor and asked what a sign from God looked like. The pastor said he wasn't sure, but he would know one if he saw one.

"Do you think," asked MacDougall, "I can raise a million dollars in a year?"

"That," said the pastor, "would be a bloody miracle."

"Then," said MacDougall, "take my dollar and give me a year. If I can raise the million, that will be your sign."

"Who do you represent?" asked the pastor.

MacDougall, who didn't represent anyone, and would have been on a date if Susan Bate hadn't leaned on him, said he represented certain business interests.

He gathered up a collection of his friends, got them to put on their best suits, which in many cases meant their only suit, and had them show up at the next meeting. The deal was done. The congregation agreed to place the matter in God's hands.

One of the people on MacDougall's committee was a single mother. A woman on welfare. When they hatched a fundraising scheme to sell brass plaques for $1000 each, she said more than anything she would love to have a plaque with her daughter's name on it. Sadly, she said, she didn't have $1000.

"You don't have to have a thousand dollars," said Jack MacDougall. "You can raise it."

And she did. In three weeks. She sold buttons for $5 each at the market. And somewhere on the back of a seat in the Imperial Theatre you can find a plaque that reads, *To my daughter, Christa, love Mom.* It was the first plaque sold. Within a year, they had sold four hundred more.

"It was that first plaque that got things going," said MacDougall. "We figured if a single mom on welfare could raise a thousand dollars, the rest of us could raise a million."

And that is more or less the way it went. One day a professor from the university, Joe Pocks, wandered into their committee room saying he would like to raise $100,000.

"I am going to run a raffle," he said. "I'll get a thousand prizes and sell a hundred thousand tickets for a dollar each."

They told him it couldn't be done. They only had a year. He would have to get three prizes donated every day for a year to get a thousand prizes. It was impossible.

Professor Pocks came back three months later with 350 prizes. He had women in old people's homes all over town knitting sweaters. Within the year he sold seventy thousand tickets for a dollar a piece.

When their year was up, the committee had raised *more than* $1 million. They bought the theatre from the church. It took another decade and more than $10 million to complete the renovation.

"All sorts of people moved in and out of the project over that decade," said MacDougall. "It was like a relay race. Lots of people carried the baton over the years."

They made it to the finish line, and like I said, the Imperial is now one great theatre.

And I will never stand on its stage again without thinking of Susan Bate and Jack MacDougall, and what you can accomplish if you set your mind to it.

4 May 2003

BIKING
ACROSS CANADA

In 1997, Cal Lane, who was living on a boat and working as a welder in Victoria, British Columbia, was accepted into the Nova Scotia School of Art and Design. This meant Cal had to cross the country somehow, and she thought that bicycle would be as good a way as any, and a lot cheaper than most. Seven flat tires and 6078 kilometres in seventy-seven days didn't change her mind.

"I'd do it again," she said. "In fact, I've been thinking about it."

And then she smiled and said, "So many memories."

I made tea.

"Tell me some of them," I said.

"Saskatchewan was the hardest," said Cal.

This might surprise some, Saskatchewan being the heart of the prairies and largely flat. I wasn't surprised. I haven't biked in Saskatchewan myself, but I have biked in Holland, so I guessed what she was talking about. Fighting a stiff wind across flat land can grind you down in a way that, well, in a way that I imagine even the Rocky Mountains wouldn't.

"That's right," said Cal. "Going up those mountains wasn't nearly as hard as I anticipated. Coming down them was harder than you'd think. You have to keep squeezing the brakes for hours on end. That can get tiring."

Cal said she biked eighty to one hundred and forty-five kilometres a day. At night, she said she and her friend Mike, who biked with her, slept wherever they were.

"We slept beside the train tracks, and once in a churchyard, and another time in a ball field behind a bar."

Cal said they got good at hiding their tent. If they felt unsure about where they were, they would set it up in a hedge where no one could see them.

"By the end," said Cal, "we were like little animals."

Sometimes, she said, she could hear deer around the tent at night. Hear them breathing and snorting. It scared her at first.

"Because I didn't know what it was," said Cal.

One night she saw fireflies for the first time.

"I was lying in the tent without the fly," she said, smiling. She thought they were stars until they started moving around. She couldn't believe her eyes.

She said the train engineers used to wave.

"They'd blow the horn and wave."

The people they met were generous.

"They gave us water and food," she said. "Even restaurants."

There was a chip wagon in Ontario where they wouldn't let Cal and Mike pay. "And it wasn't the only restaurant like that," she said.

Although Cal and Mike were travelling together, she told me they hardly talked all day. Sometimes Mike would call out and ask if she was okay, and she would squeak her dinosaur horn to say she was fine.

"Mostly," said Cal, "we just pedalled."

It was like meditation. They pedalled and pedalled. Every day that's all it was, the pedals going around and around. The pedals and the repetition of the road and the trees.

"We had no worries," said Cal. "We didn't have anything to focus on except *keep pedalling*."

She picked up her teacup and then put it down without drinking any. She stared at the cup for the longest time. Then she smiled and said, "It was so amazing to see the country like that. To see how the landscape changes. It was as if I had run my hand across the entire country like you would on a piano. I feel as if I touched it from one side to the other."

She said when she and Mike finally arrived in Halifax, they just looked at each other.

"We didn't know what to do," she said.

All they knew was how to bike. They had pedalled everywhere. They had pedalled to the store and then to their campsite.

The only injury she got on the whole trip was the day after she finished.

"I got shin splints," she said. "Because I wasn't used to walking."

When I asked her what she remembered most about her trip, Cal didn't hesitate. "The birds," she said.

"Every day you heard the same song. Over and over. It was very calming."

"It wouldn't change for weeks and weeks," she said, "and you would memorize the song. And then one day you would notice a new melody joining in and slowly, as the species changed, the new tune would take over and you would forget the old one. It was lovely."

Cal isn't the first person I know who has biked across the country and come back talking about birds. When my friend Noel told me about his bike trip across Canada, the first story he wanted to tell me was his eagle story.

Like Cal, Noel was biking from west to east. One day, around the Manitoba–Saskatchewan border, he met a man who was *walking* in the opposite direction.

Noel pulled over to the side of the road, which, of course, you never would do if you were in a car and you saw someone walking along the highway but is the only thing you *can* do if you are on a bike.

The hiker, who happened to be an Aboriginal, told Noel he had left his home in Ontario and was walking to Alberta to visit his brother. He said he had been walking for two months. He said he had lost forty pounds.

The two of them, the white cyclist from Whistler, B.C., and the Aboriginal hiker from Ontario, stood on the shoulder and bonded.

"When you drive," said Noel, "you miss the details."

"Like the caterpillars," said the hiker, "and frogs and lupins and brooks and streams."

Noel told the man that one early morning a deer had bounded through the forest, running beside him for more than a kilometre.

The man said, "Deer are important."

And then Noel told him that he had passed a dead eagle that very morning, and the man got excited and made him tell him exactly where the eagle was, so he wouldn't miss it on his way by.

Many people would think you were crazy to walk from Ontario to Alberta. But for Cal, and Noel, and that walking man, it was the point of their trips. They would tell you the best trips are the ones where you move slowly.

30 July 2006

BRIDGE WALKING

There are many reasons to celebrate bridges. Often just their scale is enough. A grand bridge, stretching across some impossible chasm, like a freight train suspended across a prairie landscape, is worthy of praise; but so, too, are all the little country bridges. The ones that make you want to pull over and climb out of your car and hang on the railing a spell.

Bridges can be beautiful for their largeness or their small-ness, but also for their straightness. Or, better, their curves. For when it is a bridge as hard as steel that is swooping and bending and rolling before your eyes, what could be more beautiful than that?

Bridges bring things together that are apart. This bank and that bank. This side and that. And that is a noble aspiration. A bridge is, above all else, a conciliator. Bridges like it when things are joined up. They favour gatherings over solitudes.

So for all these things, and of course, because almost always, there is water involved, I am in favour of bridges.

And with these things in mind, I wanted to tip my hat to the International Bridge that joins Sault Ste. Marie, Ontario, to Sault Ste. Marie, Michigan. For its beautiful curved arch trusses, and for the way it swoops and sags, and for the way they let you ride your bike from one side to the other right along with the cars. And because it has a steel railing that allows you to see the water, and because it spans the busiest shipping locks in the world—70 percent of the raw material that feeds the North American auto industry, in the form of iron ore, passes below it. This is a serious bridge.

And this June, for the twenty-third year in a row, officials are closing the bridge for an hour so that anyone who wants can walk across it. And the only reason they have for doing that is that it is a beautiful walk. Almost five kilometres long, and high enough so you can see fish in the St. Mary's River below. And a lot of other things you can't see when you are behind the wheel of a car.

So here is to the beauty of bridges. And, more to the point, to the wisdom of the bridge operators in Sault Ste. Marie, who believe in beauty and understand the importance of taking the time, from time to time, to pause and appreciate it.

28 June 2009

GETTING TO SWIFT CURRENT

At midnight, last Tuesday, after we had finished packing up the show in Yorkton, Saskatchewan, we agreed to meet in the hotel lobby at nine o'clock the next morning for the five-hour drive to Swift Current. We, being the touring cast of *The Vinyl Cafe* show: horn player Chris Whiteley, pianist John Sheard, vocalist Lisa Lindo and myself.

We assembled, a little blearily, for our complimentary hotel breakfast, packed the van and headed off——it was Day Three of the Western Tour.

Before we left Yorkton, we stopped so Chris could buy a new cable for his electric guitar. He'd left his old cable on stage in Winnipeg. We had been told McLaren's on Broadway Street should have one. So that's where we headed.

Small-town businesspeople are often called upon to use more imagination than their big-city counterparts to stay afloat. McLaren's turned out to be a monument to small-town ingenuity, a combination music store, trophy outlet and supplier of medical provisions. We could have walked out of McLaren's with an upright piano, a surgical syringe and a silver-plated bowling trophy. We settled for the amp chord and a handful of guitar picks. And we left town.

We were almost immediately onto the prairie, floating along a highway that was so straight and empty that John, who was driving, could have tied off the steering wheel to the rear-view mirror and done his morning crossword.

We rolled by kilometres of empty fields under a sky so low and grey that it felt like snow. At this time of year, the prairie landscape is drawn from a pallet of beige and browns—a beautiful and contemplative vista.

I was in the back of the van, with my head down, clicking away at my laptop, answering emails, when a train whistle split the air. John whooped.

"I waved at the guy," he said, "and he blew the whistle."

He was still beaming a few minutes later.

"He blew the whistle for me," he repeated.

We were all smiling now. The freight, so elemental to the prairie that it seemed part of the natural world, was still rocking along beside us. What is it about trains that turn us into children?

An hour and three freights later, we passed a field of wheat stubble inundated with black-and-white birds. Thousands and thousands of birds. There were more birds in the field than I had ever seen in one place in my life. They might have been magpies; they were too far away for me to identify.

Maybe I had been in the van too long. Or maybe it was my turn to touch my childhood. Whatever. I barked at John to pull over.

The van was a kilometre and a half down the road before John understood I was serious. When he realized I was, he turned around, and we backtracked that kilometre and a half and parked on the gravel shoulder. The birds were maybe a half-kilometre from the highway. Unable to get anyone to join me, I slipped alone under the strand of barbed wire that bordered the road, and I began to lope across the prairie like a dog. I wanted to make it into the middle of the flock before the birds took off. I wanted to feel the surge of their wings all around me. I thought the sound would be incredible.

I didn't even get close before a skittish character squawked into the sky and took everyone else with him. The birds rose into the air like a shook carpet. I returned to the van, disappointed.

Our next stop was at a gas station in the Qu'Appelle River Valley, which like all river valleys in Saskatchewan appears dramatically and, seemingly, out of nowhere. You think it is flat forever when suddenly the land folds, and opens, and there is water, and hills, and stands of trees.

Saskatchewan river valleys make me think of the times before Europeans arrived. I imagine First Nations people moving through the landscape.

We stopped a while later in Enfold, looking for gas and coffee, and realized we weren't going to find either. We climbed out of the van and saw all the businesses in the small country town had been long abandoned, and that many of the clapboard houses were empty too—another farming community on its way to becoming a ghost town. As the farms get bigger, the towns get smaller. The wind was blowing. We stood there, looking around.

Someone said, "All this is going to blow away one day."

We climbed back into the van and headed off again onto the highway with Swift Current in our sights.

28 November 1999

PRAIRIE WIND

Art Grenville farms bison about an hour to the north and east of Rosebud, Alberta, in a part of the country where you can feel as if you're standing close to history just about anywhere you are.

On my way to his place, I pulled over and walked through a roadside graveyard. Standing among the tombstones and dwarfed by the flat-bottomed thunderclouds ranging the edge of the sky, I felt as if I was standing in a painting by William Kurelek. It was good to be back in a part of the country where the view allowed thunderclouds and blue sky to share the same horizon—on the very edge of the prairie, the place where the earth opens and the Canadian Badlands begin. The topography is almost biblical, and brings to mind the cradle of creation.

Before I left, I had checked a book to clear up the difference between a buffalo and a bison. A buffalo is a water buffalo. We don't have those. We might be used to calling what we do have "buffalo," but the horned and heavy-humped animals that roamed North America in impossible numbers before Europeans arrived to slaughter them into almost extinction are, correctly, bison.

When I arrived at his bison farm, Art suggested we take the tractor out to the pasture, where he keeps part of his herd.

There is something quite indescribable about finding yourself standing on a prairie hill surrounded by bison. It could be all the movies I've seen, or maybe the pictures in the history books, or maybe I'm just a romantic, but a herd of bison seems to fit into the landscape in an organic way that a herd of cattle doesn't. The bison seem to be *of* the land rather than just on it. Standing amid them made me feel as if I were of the land too.

As we stood there silently, Art Grenville pulled a book out of his coat pocket and asked if it was okay if he read a passage out loud. It was Peter Fidler's journal. Fidler was a geographer and contemporary of the great, and better known, David Thompson. Fidler travelled with the Piegans to the valley of the Red Deer River in the late 1700s, and it is his account of the bison, or, buffalo, as Fidler calls them, (no wonder we have been confused for centuries) that Art Grenville wanted to read to me.

It wasn't Fidler's description, however, that I found remarkable. I've heard similar accounts before, about how the plains were so thick with bison that you couldn't see the ground for ten miles all around you. It was something that Art did when he had finished reading that affected me. He put the book back in his pocket, pointed off to the southwest and said, "I figure Fidler was standing on *that* ridge there when he wrote that." Grenville was talking about something that was written more than two hundred years ago.

"I figure," he said, "that the view was pretty much the same."

Only once before have I felt so close to history. That, too, was on these dry and rolling plains. It was the night, some decades ago, in the Cypress Hills, when I stood alone listening to a songbird swooping and felt the ghost of the great Indian warrior Sitting Bull, who crossed over the Medicine Line into the North West Territories, as they were then called, seeking refuge from the American cavalry who were pursuing him after the Battle of the Little Big Horn.

The dry winds that blow the sage bush over this parched and cracked prairie carry stories you can sometimes almost touch.

The trick is to be there when the wind is blowing. And to listen to the soft whispers of the dry grass when it does.

7 May 2006

PARLIAMENT HILL

The first thing I did on Monday morning, with time on my hands, was what I always do when I have time on my hands in the nation's capital. I got in a taxi and asked the driver to take me to Parliament Hill. I find the Parliament Buildings, both in their stony reality, and for all that they symbolize, an inspiring place. I am moved by all of it—by the certainty of the stone and the symmetry of the architecture, by the fragility of the eternal flame and the aspirations of the Peace Tower, by the languid lawn at the front door and the rapid river at the back. Even if I don't have time to stop by, I like to *drive* by and pay my respects. *Take the long way,* I always tell my taxi driver, even if I am hurrying to the airport.

This week I was *not* hurrying. I had time. But that's not all I had. My friend David McCormick, who is a member of the Ottawa Press Gallery, had arranged to get me a press pass. For the first time in thirty years I was going to be able to wander wherever I wanted.

The pass came with instructions. "There are two hidden gems," said David, who knows my taste in these things. "I think you should see them."

He told me to go to the Parliamentary Library. "There is

an inkwell on display," he explained. "It was used at the Charlottetown Conference of 1864. And then again, eighty-five years later, for the signing of the terms of union under which Newfoundland joined the Canadian federation."

"I will check the inkwell out," I promised.

"When you do," said David, "check out the cake too."

"The cake?" I replied.

"There is a cake on display. It was baked by the parliamentary kitchen more than thirty years ago, for the library's one hundredth anniversary You have to see it."

"Why?" I asked.

"Because it was baked in the shape of the library," said David. "It is the oddest thing, but affecting in an odd way."

An inkwell and a cake. These are the sort of things that I love. *Let the tourists climb the Peace Tower,* I thought as I walked along Wellington Street. *Let the students of politics head for the House of Commons. I will go to the library, and in that most splendid of Parliament's many splendid rooms, in the wood-lined cathedral of books, I will pray at a familiar altar, the altar of the inconsequential.*

I have always believed that the big truths are hidden in the small things. An inkwell struck me as such a nice small thing. The indelible smell of ink, like the smell of blood, or the smell of the sea, recalls elemental things. The alchemy of liquid that, with the stroke of a pen, can become law.

I was touched that someone had had enough respect for history to guard that inkwell for nearly one hundred years so that it could be used during both the first and most recent days of Confederation, and I was pleased that I was going to find it displayed so modestly, on a library desk.

And so I thanked David, and I picked up my pass with great anticipation.

If you have never been to the Parliament Buildings, the best way to walk into the Centre Block is to imagine yourself walking into a cathedral. It is all limestone marble and gothic arches, bathed in the soft light of a setting sun, or as the parliamentarians would have us believe, I am certain, an approaching dawn. You wouldn't be surprised as you walked around to spot a red-cloaked bishop padding down one of the corridors, or I wouldn't. Like one of Canada's grand railway hotels, Parliament is all history and tradition.

I wandered into the Centre Block, into the Rotunda, and then down the Hall of Honour heading to the Library of Parliament.

Before I got there, however, I was drawn to another corridor—one that the public isn't supposed to use. It is reserved for members who want to slip out the back door of Parliament when they are trying to avoid people like me. And there, tucked away in a small alcove, I stumbled on a sculpture, a small bust by the great French artist and father of modern sculpture Auguste Rodin.

To Canada, reads the plaque on the pedestal, *whose sons shed their blood to safeguard world freedom.*

The plaque is signed, *from grateful France.*

I am moved by grand gestures made with modesty. By small, determined things.

On I went, and soon enough came to the library, where Irene Brown, the librarian on duty, told me with obvious disappointment that the cake I had been sent to see had begun to crumble and was no longer on display. The inkwell was gone too. It was in storage.

Irene was soon joined by her colleague, a librarian named Louis, and with the spontaneous enthusiasm typical of librarians everywhere, they soon enough had set aside their work and joined me in mine.

"We could show you our favourite *book*," said Irene.

"What book is that?" I asked.

"It was sent to Canada by Queen Victoria," said Irene. "After the death of her husband."

"Yes," says Louis. "It is a collection of the Prince Consort's speeches. It is inscribed in the Queen's hand."

"What does the inscription say?" I asked.

"To the Library of Parliament," said Louis.

"From a heartbroken widow," added Irene.

I passed a pleasant hour in the library before saying my goodbyes and continuing my wanderings.

I headed up to the top floor, the sixth floor, to the parliamentary restaurant, which I have always wanted to see. The maître d', a woman named Margueritte, welcomed me just as graciously as the librarians had.

"That table *there*," she said, pointing at an alcove near the door, "is reserved for the *prime minister. That* alcove is for Conservative members, *that* one for Liberals and *that* is where the NDP gather."

Then, sensing my interest, she said, "Would you like to see the New Zealand Room?"

She took me to the back of the restaurant and into a small and elegant dining room with a table that would sit a dozen, but not one more.

"It is panelled with wood sent by New Zealand after the Centre Block burned to the ground in 1916," she said.

And it was at this moment, as I stood there under the green copper roof of Parliament, in that modest dining room with its magnificent view of the Ottawa River, that I had my little epiphany.

One hundred years ago New Zealand was pretty much on the far side of the moon as far as Canada was concerned. And vice versa. Yet, in 1916 someone in New Zealand heard that our Parliament Buildings had burned to the ground, and they responded to that news in such an odd yet peculiarly appropriate way.

They sent wood. To Canada, of all places. As if wood was something Canada was lacking. And someone here received that gift with the respect with which it was given. And those two small acts of respect had served the greater good.

And it occurred to me, as I stood there all these years later, in what is now known as the New Zealand Room, that we have lost our understanding of that sort of respect.

In its place we have developed an impulse for cynicism. Too quickly we look at our politics and our politicians as if everything was easy to figure out; as if compromises didn't have to be made; as if you can always say exactly what you mean; as if a thoughtful person can't reflect on something and then change his or her mind; as if the business of governing isn't complicated.

Cynicism is an easy place to pitch a tent. And it is worth remembering, when we are tempted by that soft and undemanding clearing in the forest, that there are more noble campsites.

Parliament has been, and could still be, the best of us. And, I would put forward, it behooves us to embrace that possibility, to admit to that possibility, to own that possibility and, most importantly, to expect it. These are important days. This is an important place. We owe it many things. Our passions, our commitments, our truths and, yes, our respect. The broken-hearted Queen Victoria showed that when she signed and sent that book in the memory of her husband. Auguste Rodin showed it as he fashioned that sculpture for all of France. Those New Zealanders showed it as they bundled together their little shipment of wood. Those librarians show it as they guard that inkwell still. And so should we, each one of us, as we come together in our todays and our tomorrows, to consider, as best we can, the great questions of our times.

13 September 2009

MAYNARD HELMER

Orma Melvin met Maynard Helmer in September 1946 on the first day of school. She met him in the village of Winchester, a small farming community set in the heart of Ontario's dairy country, halfway between Ottawa and Morrisburg.

Orma was neither born nor raised in Winchester. She arrived by train on Labour Day weekend that year. She was twenty-three years old and fresh out of the Ontario College of Education, with a contract to teach English, French and physical education at the Winchester High School. The school board had arranged a boarding house for Orma. She went straight there from the station and hung up her new grey seersucker dress, which she had bought at Holt's. The next morning she put on her new dress and a pair of white chamoisette gloves and set off for school. It was her first real job, and she was scared stiff. She had barely walked a block when a young man appeared and began to dance around her. As he danced, he sang.

"Son of a B, drunker than hell. Son of a B, drunker than Hell."

Orma didn't understand what he meant. But she did understand that he didn't mean harm. So she kept walking, and he kept dancing. He seemed to her to be loosely put together. His clothes and his limbs all seemed unstrung. He followed her all the way to school, dancing around her the whole time. Singing the whole time too.

"Son of a B, drunker than Hell."

When they arrived at school, however, he didn't follow her in.

That was Orma's introduction to Maynard Helmer. She soon learned that Maynard was what we now call a child with developmental disabilities. Orma learned that Maynard attended school for a few years, and although the teachers and the students were kind to him, his academic career wasn't successful. Maynard never progressed beyond grade two.

In the 1940s, there was no place for a boy like Maynard in a town like Winchester. But Maynard's father, Cy, didn't want his son to be institutionalized in a big city. So Maynard stayed in Winchester all his life.

In the ten years she lived in town, Orma got to know him. It was hard not to. Maynard was a fixture in the village. Every morning he made the rounds of all the cafés. He knew everyone, and everyone knew him. He'd go to Mary's, and Sutton's, and Alexander's Lunch. By the time the five o'clock whistle blew at the Ault's Dairy, which was Maynard's signal to huff down Main Street and get home for dinner, he had drunk about twenty-five cups of coffee. He probably didn't pay for one of them.

"What you doing today, Maynard?"

"Busy," he'd say. "Busy. Busy. Busy. Lots of things to do today. Lots of things to do."

If there was any job going on around town, Maynard would be there. If someone was digging a hole for a fencepost in the most remote corner of the village, Maynard would show up before the first shovel load of dirt hit the ground.

If there was a wedding or a funeral, Maynard would often be standing at the door with the minister at the end of the service, shaking hands with everyone as they left the church.

His grandfather Herb Helmer was one of the village's first police officers. People will tell you that it was something to see old Herb Helmer and Maynard walking down Main Street together. They'll tell you that there was something about the old man's walk, something about the way he put his arm around Maynard's shoulder. Maynard took to wearing a police hat and carrying a black notebook wherever he went. When Gibb Raistrick became the chief, Gibb took him under his wing, and Maynard kept tagging along. No one in Winchester was surprised if Gibb drove up on official police business, and Maynard climbed out of the car with him, pulling his notebook out of his pocket. Maynard took his police duties seriously.

If he was walking down St. Lawrence, and he saw a car that he thought was travelling too fast, Maynard would pull out his book and say, "That's going to cost that son of a bitch twenty dollars."

And he would scratch something down in his notebook. Maynard couldn't write, of course. But he was always referring to his book or scribbling something in it.

He loved to direct traffic. Sometimes, if there was an accident, or the mood seized him, he would get out in the middle of Main Street and he'd wave at the cars like his grandfather Herb. People would wave back and do just what he told them. Everyone in town had time for Maynard. So what if it took five more minutes to get to the drugstore?

It is hard for someone living in a big city to appreciate how the entire village took Maynard into their hearts. He rode the fire engine in every Santa Claus parade. People came out to see Maynard as much as they came out to see anything else.

They gave him a white hard hat that said *The Boss* in black letters on the front. He loved to be the boss. He'd be out at the arena straightening things up for Frank Morgan and he'd stop.

"I'm the boss, aren't I, Frank?" he'd say.

"Oh yes, you are Mayne boy. You're the Big Boss," said Frank.

In 1970, when the village was putting in sewers and the truck drivers from Morrisburg arrived with their loads of gravel and sand, it was Maynard who met them.

He said, "Yeah, you just dump that load over there. And you put that one there." When the foreman arrived and started yelling at the drivers, asking them what they hell they were doing, they pointed at Maynard and said, "The Boss told us to put it there."

When Shirley Fawcett's daughter had a baby, Maynard showed up at the hospital with a stuffed toy. Shirley remembers him standing arm's length from the bassinette, reaching over to slip the toy in, and adjusting it so the baby could see it. Then he stepped back again and stood there, smiling.

The doctor said he never progressed much beyond the mental capacity of a six-year-old. Yet everyone in Winchester will tell you that Maynard had an amazing memory, especially for faces. They'll tell you that Lois Coones left town as a young woman and didn't come back for thirty-five or forty years, and when he saw her, Maynard said, "Hi, Coones. Where you been? What are you doing?"

People didn't just put up with Maynard. He was part of their town. Part of their lives. Sometimes Maynard would bring his electric razor downtown, and Gibb would help him shave. Sometimes he would bring his tie. Maynard liked ties, especially bow ties, which he wore nearly every day, with plain shirts and plaid shirts—made no difference to Maynard. He loved to dress up, and he loved it when people told him he was looking good.

Every year at Christmas, Maynard went home with more gifts than anyone else in town. He would have to go home two or three times a day with his arms full of presents.

People invited him to their homes. They shared special occasions with him.

Joel Steele, who runs the Country Boy Men's Wear, remembers the day Roy Fawcett came in the store and said that Maynard was coming to his daughter's wedding.

"I want to get him a suit," said Roy. "And I want to get him a nice one." They chose the best one in the store. They split the cost.

When Maynard got sick, Frank Morgan put it in his column in the paper, and Maynard got hundreds of cards—mailbags full of cards, from all over the country, even from the States, from people who had moved away, from people who heard that Maynard was in the hospital.

Orma had not had a lot to do with Maynard since 1955, when she left Winchester with her husband, until this April, when she came back to the village for a funeral.

It was a miserable and rainy day. As she drove through town, Orma noticed a lot of changes. The old school where she had taught had burned down. There was a new park on the corner of St. Lawrence and Main, with a little bandshell. She mentioned the park and the bandshell to Rob Preston after the funeral.

"It's a lovely looking park," she said.

"Did you read the plaque?" asked Rob.

"No." said Orma. She hadn't read the plaque. What did it say?

Rob wouldn't tell her.

"You have to read it yourself," he said.

"Come on," said Orma. "It's pouring rain."

"Don't leave town without reading the plaque," said Rob.

So on the way home Orma made her son drive her to the centre of town. She got out in the middle of that April storm, walked up to the bandshell and read the plaque. She felt tears well up in her eyes as she read it.

In memory of Maynard Helmer, it read. *This was his town. This was his corner. These were his people.*

Maynard's mother died when he was young boy. He was raised by his father. Cy Helmer liked a drink. It was Cy who was "drunker than hell" that morning that Orma first met Maynard. When Cy died, one of Maynard's cousins, Audrey Robinson, from Iroquois, agreed to look after Maynard. Audrey was not a wealthy woman. For years she and Maynard got by on what little she had and on her late husband's army pension.

A year before Maynard got sick, Audrey won the lottery. She had a half of a ticket that was worth $1.9 million.

She bought a new house, and everything was going fine until Maynard got sick and went to hospital. His room in the hospital had everything: balloons, and flowers, and cards, and visitors. There were always visitors. Frank Morgan was there the day he died. He had gone to pick Maynard up in the morning. He was going to take him downtown so he could have coffee with the boys. Maynard was so excited he had woken up at five o'clock in the morning, but just as they were going for the car, he took a turn for the worse and they couldn't go. He died around supper. That was 1990.

There was a mob at Maynard's funeral. Hundreds of people came.

About a year later, Frank Morgan at the arena thought they should do something to remember Maynard. He went to Audrey, and she agreed. She took some of her lottery winnings and gave them to the village, and they built the bandshell at the corner of St. Lawrence and Main.

There was a mob there the night it opened too. Frank Morgan was the master of ceremonies. The local Members of Parliament, both provincial and federal, were there. Shirley Fawcett cried. Lots of people cried.

It has been there four years now, but it looks like it's been there forever. And if you happen to be driving by Winchester on a Friday evening this summer, and you have some time to kill, I'm sure the people of the village wouldn't mind if you stopped to have a look. They have a concert planned for the bandshell every Friday night of the summer. They start at eight o'clock, and sometimes there are as many as two hundred people out to listen. A lot of people bring lawn chairs with them. They put them down on the corner of Main and St. Lawrence, which used to be Maynard's favourite corner, right there in the centre of the village where he could keep track of everything.

1 August 1994

MOTELS

The roadside motel has fallen into disfavour these days and that is a shame. I am talking about the kind of place you can still stumble upon if you are prepared to give up the highway and the notion of making good time. You find them lingering on the edge of summer towns, with twenty rooms and a pink-and-green neon sign that buzzes and says *Vacancy* when you pull up, thank God. The kind of place that closes in the winter because the owners who live in the mysterious rooms behind the office go to Florida. When you check in they give you a key on a brown melamine key ring that says Room Six, but you park your car in front of Room Eight, because the spot in front of Room Six is already taken by a car with Michigan licence plates—a family of seven whom your kids will meet by the pool, and who, you will learn, are heading home from a wedding in some town that you won't remember, but it must have been sunny there because their kids are all sunburned.

That's the kind of place I am missing.

The kind of place you stay at when you are driving farther than any sane person would in a day, especially with a backseat full of kids, and you stay there partly because they have an outdoor pool but mostly because of the giant statue of the squirrel by the sign. And you were happy to stop, happy to send the kids to the motel office by themselves for ice and happy to sit at the picnic table by the poolside, with your beer, watching them do cannonballs.

And later on, after they warm up, and you've eaten dinner at the place down the road (you'll have the fried clams), everyone will watch TV together from the two beds, and the thought will cross your mind that this might just be the highlight of the entire vacation. There, at the motel on the edge of the highway with the statue of the giant squirrel, because all these years later, even though your parents took you to Stratford to see Shakespeare, and to the Canadian National Exhibition to see the butter sculpture, and to more museums than anyone could possibly be expected to care about, and to PEI and Nova Scotia, and the coast of Maine, and one summer to England, even after all that, the things you remember with the greatest fondness are those moments when dusk had settled, and you were in the back of the car hanging over the seat, and your father announced you should start looking for a place, and it was understood it would have a pool, and be within earshot of the highway, and for breakfast you would have cereal that came in one of those single-serving boxes you break open on the side and use as a bowl.

And that's just the beginning of it, because another thing about family car trips, along with a mother who can pull things out of her purse as if it was an Advent calendar, and goofy alphabet songs, and signs you hold up to other cars that say things like *Honk if you think my dad needs a haircut*, the other thing about hitting the road in July or August is that the family food rules tend to go right out the window.

Roadside motels are only ever your destination if you are actually *on the road*. And what better way to be on the road than to find yourself on a summer evening, in an overpacked car, surrounded by the people you love.

30 July 2006

MEETING FAMOUS PEOPLE

Sitting in the Halifax airport, eating a sandwich and with an hour to kill between planes, I heard an announcement that caught my attention. "Would Cindy Crawford please report to the information booth on the main floor."

Well now, I thought, putting my sandwich down and looking up from my magazine. *What should I do about this?* It's not every day you have an opportunity to see a supermodel in the flesh. I wondered about my next step—should I really get up, leave the departure area and check this out? I had the time. As I wondered about what to do, I recalled another morning at another airport in Atlantic Canada—the morning I had gone into the men's room and walked into a man the size of a furnace, realizing only when I got back to the departure lounge and looked around that I was sharing the airport with an army of big guys. I don't know what the collective noun for a group of wrestlers is: a *fall* of wrestlers? A *smash* of wrestlers? A *scream* of wrestlers? Whatever the case, the Charlottetown departure lounge, not the largest lounge in the country, was chockablock with wrestlers. And it didn't take me long to figure out that these weren't just any wrestlers. These guys were the pride of the WWF: Rowdy Randy Piper,

Hulk Hogan, Jake the Snake, all of them half asleep and waiting to be stuffed onto a plane to God knows what next stop along the road.

At the time I was on tour myself, promoting my first collection of *Vinyl Cafe* stories. I was carrying a copy of the book with me that I was asking other authors to sign when we met at readings. I had all sorts of great signatures in my book, including actor Nick Nolte, who I had run into in the lobby of the Ritz-Carlton Hotel in Montreal.

I love that book, and the memories it holds, and I have always regretted that I was too shy to ask Hulk Hogan to add his signature that morning. He looked so tired. I didn't want to disturb him.

But here I was, four years later, back in another East Coast airport, with a chance to snag Cindy Crawford. Of course, maybe it wasn't the real Cindy Crawford. Maybe it was just a coincidence. Maybe it was someone with the same name. That can happen to a person.

One Sunday morning, many summers ago, I headed off on a bike ride in downtown Toronto and ended up pedalling along the Humber River Valley.

There is a boat club down there, a kind of rundown and seedy club, or it was at the time, which would be the only kind of boat club I could imagine myself joining. I stopped and was admiring one boat, fantasizing about life on the water, when the owner's head suddenly popped through the deck, like a water rat, followed by his body, a smile and an invitation to join him on board. He toured me around his boat proudly, and we exchanged pleasantries, and as I was climbing back onto the dock, I turned and held out my hand and said, "Thanks for the tour. My name is Stuart McLean."

He smiled, nodded, shook my hand and then, fixing me with his eyes, said, in a distinctly Scottish brogue, "Pleased to meet you, Stuart. My name is *Ronald Macdonald.*"

I tried my best not to react. I tried not to blink. He was, maybe, sixty-five years old. I left him thinking how it was possible to go through an entire life with a perfectly normal name, and then one day, turn fifty and get hit from behind.

I had a student once, at Ryerson University; his name was, still is, Peter Duck. He is a talented young reporter. Peter Duck's grandfather lived the first twelve years of his life with the perfectly normal name Donald.

So maybe the Cindy Crawford who was being paged to the information desk at the Halifax Airport was not Cindy Crawford the supermodel. Maybe she was a different, less glamorous Cindy Crawford. A Cindy, all things considered, whom I would probably be happier to know.

Or maybe it was a joke. I read in a magazine that John Kennedy Junior's friends, who were fond of teasing him about his perfect hair, once arranged for *helmet head* to be paged at some airport or other. According to the article, he answered the page.

And the question now was whether I was going to answer the call for Cindy or, like I had when Hulk Hogan was in my grasp, let her slip away.

I checked the departure board for the flights scheduled to leave in the next hour. Except for my flight to Toronto, they were all going to small towns. She'll be on my flight, I reasoned. Where else could she be going?

I think that was her in seat 3C, cleverly disguised as a middle-aged schoolteacher. In the end I let her sit there alone. She looked too tired to bother.

26 September 1999

MAXINE MONTGOMERY

My friend Jill was flying west, on her way to Vancouver and not in a hurry. The kids were in camp, and Jill was in possession of the greatest thing *anyone* can possess during the dog days of summer. She had time on her hands.

And that meant when she made her booking, Jill decided to save a bit of money. She chose the *cheapest* of the flights going west, the one that included the three-hour layover in Saskatoon, Saskatchewan.

Not only would this flight save money, it meant she might also get to see the prairie. Jill hadn't seen the prairie in years.

Everything went as planned. Before she knew it, Jill had finished the first leg of her trip, cleared security and found herself standing in the John G. Diefenbaker International Airport—a modest place as these places go. Her luggage had been checked through to Vancouver. So Jill was footloose, with nothing to do but weigh her options. There seemed to be two. She could climb into a taxi and say, "To the prairie, my fine fellow, and make haste." Or she could rent a car and see if she could find the great plains herself. It shouldn't be hard. She figured she could choose a course, any course, hold it and she would get there eventually. Unsure which would be the most prudent course of action, Jill decided to seek advice. She turned to a woman who seemed to be there to answer just such a question—the friendly looking woman at the *Saskatoon Shines* booth. Jill smiled. The woman smiled back. And so, encouraged, Jill approached the booth and explained how she was between flights, and how she had hoped she could use the time to *see the prairie*.

"I just want to stand in a field of wheat," she said.

Should she take a taxi or rent a car?

Jill was talking to Maxine Montgomery, one of the managers at the Saskatoon Airport Authority, who just happened to be at the booth that morning. Wanting to stand in a field of wheat struck Maxine as a perfectly natural thing to do. She looked Jill over and said, "Can you drive standard?"

Jill nodded yes.

Maxine said, "Well then, why don't you just take *my* car?"

The next thing Jill knew, she was driving Maxine's silver Acura under a big blue sky, sailing along past fields of canola and young green wheat, with sweet air drifting in the sunroof and Neil Young on the radio.

Hearing about that made me almost as happy as it made her then.

God bless Maxine Montgomery, I thought, *for extending the unexpected kindness of a stranger. And God bless Jill, for taking the long way around.*

I don't know who taught us to be in such a hurry these days. I don't know why, or when, it became so important, when we are going from here to there, to do it as fast as humanly possible. It is a sorry state of affairs. You can't blame the airlines. The airlines do their bit. They always *offer* a long way around. You can *always* go via Saskatoon, and usually, if you do, they charge you less for the privilege.

It should be no surprise that I am in favour of the side roads. And the forgotten art of dawdling. So here's to Maxine Montgomery. And here's to the much-maligned layover. From now on I am going to do my best to incorporate a few into each and every day. So if you call to ask me over, you'll know what I mean when I say it might take a while, that I am coming, but I am coming via Saskatoon.

21 September 2008

GANDER INTERNATIONAL AIRPORT

Gander, Newfoundland, is the only town I know that was built as a *result* of an airport. Everywhere else, it happened the other way around. Everywhere else, the town came first. But not in Gander.

They carved the Gander Airport out of the Newfoundland forest *before* there was a town, or even close to a town. The airport came in the 1930s. The town came two decades later.

Today, Gander is a substantial little place. There is a Canadian Tire and a grocery store—as well stocked as the ones in the city where I live—and a Tim Hortons, of course. But no one would ever say Gander is a big city. The local phone book fills fewer than twenty pages. The town is still a chin-up away from ten thousand people.

Yet there was a time when the Gander Airport was the largest airport *in the world*. Bigger than LaGuardia and Idlewild, bigger than Gatwick and Heathrow, and arguably more important than any of them.

The runways at Gander are so big that they are still one of the alternate landing sites for the space shuttle. But I'm getting ahead of myself. I should back up a bit. I should begin where any storyteller worth his salt begins. I should begin at the beginning.

In 1937, Gander was no more than mile 213 on the trans-island railway, a milepost in the wilderness, in the middle of a rock, in the middle of the ocean—which doesn't sound like a spot to build anything, let alone the largest airport in the world. But suddenly mile 213 found itself precisely at the centre of the world.

If you draw a straight line from New York to London, you go right over Gander, and back in those days if you wanted to fly along that line, you needed a place to put down to refuel. So with an eye to the future they carved the airport out of the woods.

And then, almost as if it was planned, the war came along. So they made the runways longer.

It is hard to overstate the importance of the Gander airport to the war effort. The Allies would have won World War II without the Gander airport, but the war was shorter because of it.

Pretty much everyone in Gander will tell you that Frank Tibbo knows more about the airport's history than anyone else alive. I sat in his basement late one afternoon and he gave me a history lesson. During the war, twenty thousand fighters and heavy bombers, built in North America, were brought to Gander and flown across the Atlantic to the United Kingdom. At the beginning of the war, they were shipping planes by sea, said Frank, and losing as much as 80 percent of the shipments to German U-boats. No one believed they could fly over; they didn't have the range. Frank shook his head and told me that they hadn't counted on the engineers who modified the fuel tanks, or the bush pilots and crop dusters who flew the planes. Often by dead reckoning. The first flight of seven Lockheed Hudsons left on 10 November 1940.

What a story. They were supposed to leave the day before, but there was so much ice on the planes they couldn't scrape it off. So they waited a day. There was only one *real* navigator among the seven planes. So instructions were simple: *if you get separated, head for England.* They did get separated. They hit bad weather. But they all made it.

By the end of the war, planes flying out of Gander were guarding convoys, ferreting out submarines and, of course, being ferried to England not by the tens but by the hundreds every week.

And then, when the war was over, the airport was right at the epicentre of civilian flight. If you were flying east from Paris, you might stop at Cairo, Constantinople or Karachi. You might even overnight at the world famous Raffles hotel in Singapore.

If you were flying from New York to London, you put down in Gander. Virtually every plane that flew across the Atlantic stopped in. In 1956, which was the heyday of it all, approximately one hundred and fifty international flights put down at Gander airport *every single day.*

And something remarkable happened. Someone, somewhere, realized that the international transit lounge at the Gander International Airport might be, probably would be, the only impression of Canada that thousands of people ever had.

If Canada was going to make a good impression, *this* was her only chance.

So they decided to build a showcase. They commissioned a lounge to end all lounges, with a geometric terrazzo floor from Italy, sleek mid-century modern furniture from the über design house Herman Miller. And a stunning seventy-two-foot mural—an ode to flight—painted on site. The artist, Kenneth Lochhead, from the Canadian prairies, used more than five hundred dozen eggs to temper his paint.

It was a remarkable room—an avant-guard snapshot of the future when it was designed and appointed, and today, a glorious snapshot of the past, because what is most remarkable of all is that the Gander Airport International Lounge has remained virtually untouched for fifty years.

The *New York Times Style Magazine* was impressed enough to commission a feature about the lounge. In the glowing essay, the article quoted Alan C. Elder, curator at the Canadian Museum of Civilization, who said the lounge is "one of the most beautiful and most important Modernist rooms in the country. Maybe, the most important room."

I was born at the edge of the age of aviation, the era of airlines and airships, jet planes and rockets, the astonishment of flight defined my boyhood. And so when I read that article, I bought a ticket and took myself to Gander.

I spent an afternoon at the airport, and here's what I can add to Elder's enthusiasm. I think the lounge is one of the most remarkable rooms I have ever been to in Canada, every bit as glorious as some of the grand railway hotels and stations this country is known for.

And in better shape than most. The lounge feels as if they closed the doors in 1959 and only reopened them yesterday.

And its history is almost as splendid as its design. Because if every plane that crossed the Atlantic put down there, so did every person.

"Oh sure," said Cynthia Goodyear, whom I met in the airport restaurant, and who has worked there, at various jobs, for twenty-seven years.

"I have served all the presidents, from Ronald Reagan to George W. Bush."

And to heck with the presidents, Cynthia has made tea for the Queen.

"That's right," she said. "But she turned it down. She asked for coffee instead. Cream, no sugar."

Just about everyone in town has a story like that.

"That's true," said Marilyn Stuckless, who was a teenager when Fidel Castro came through town and went tobogganing for the first, and probably *only,* time in his life.

"There were a bunch of us on the hill opposite the Hotel Gander," said Marilyn. "And these men came along. They were more tanned than us, that's for sure. And excited too. They told us it was the first time they had seen snow."

Someone told *me* that when Fidel went down the hill on his borrowed toboggan, he had a cigar in his mouth.

"I don't remember a cigar," said Marilyn. "But that was a long time ago."

A more innocent time. Before air travellers were shuffled through X-ray machines and cordoned off behind security glass. In those days you didn't need a ticket to get into the lounge; you could just walk in, and on Sunday afternoons that's what townsfolk would do. They would drive out to the airport and get an ice cream and hang out in the lounge and chat with Muhammad Ali. Everyone from that era has an autograph or two. If you had made it your life's work to collect autographs in the Gander airport, if that was the only job you ever did, and you were good at it, you could have retired wealthy.

The list of the people who went through the lounge reads like a social register of the twentieth century. Everyone thinks The Beatles' first stop in North America was New York City. Everybody is wrong—their first stop was Gander. Jackie O stopped there. And so did Frank Sinatra, Winston Churchill, Nikita Khrushchev, Marlene Dietrich, Richard Nixon, Richard Burton, Elizabeth Taylor, Ingrid Bergman, Julia Roberts, Tom Cruise and John Travolta, who still drops in regularly on his own plane. Humphrey Bogart, Bob Hope, Tiger Woods, Woody Allen, Bruce Willis, Demi Moore, Rod Stewart, Clint Eastwood.

"I know a lot of them personally," said Cynthia. "Elizabeth Taylor always calls ahead and asks for our homemade bread. Vicente Fox orders two plates of lasagna."

"Bill Clinton loves our muffins," said the man standing beside Cynthia. "I saw him stuff a few in his pocket on his way out."

The Gander International Airport is not as busy as it once was.

A lot of the flights that land these days are private flights. Corporate planes. These days there are no more than five scheduled flights landing every day.

As for international flights, today's jets don't need to refuel on their way back and forth to Europe. Eleven international flights put down in Gander the month I visited.

These days the flights that do stop are often unscheduled.

When they arrive, phones start ringing around town. And in this world where customer service is often an automated voice message, people in Gander tumble out of bed in the middle of the night and open up the gift shop and staff the restaurant and the duty free. They stand by, ready to serve.

They are still rolling out the red carpet to people from all over the world in Gander, and they will roll it out at any hour of the day or night.

That is how it all began during the war. And during the early days of transatlantic flight. And on September 11, 2001, when almost forty planes landed out of the blue. And everyone was cared for.

Canadians like to see themselves as a nation that welcomes others.

That is what they do in Gander.

They have been doing it for years.

In style.

28 March 2010

MY FAVOURITE PHOTOGRAPH

Whenever I am in Victoria, British Columbia, and have time to spare, I drop in to visit my friend Jim Munro. Jim owns and operates Munro's books on Government Street, in that beautiful old part of Victoria down by the water.

Munro's is a wonderful bookstore, one of the last great independent bookstores in the country, and for years and years, for decades, one of the best. It is certainly one of the best appointed; housed in a glorious old bank, Munro's was big before the big chains arrived and made big the name of the game where bookstores are concerned. But it is not for its size, or its knowledgeable staff, or its well-stocked shelves that I like to visit Munro's, although those would all be good reasons. Truth be told, there are other bookstores in Victoria that could fit that bill; there is a good Chapters down the street, and Bolen Books across town, and Renaissance Books on Bastion Square, which is as good a second-hand book-store as you will find anywhere. In fact, if it's bookstores you are looking for, Victoria is as good a place to go as anywhere.

The thing is, it is not the books, or even Jim Munro's always convivial welcome, that draws me to Munro's. I like to go because, when I do, I can always pop into Jim's office and spend a moment with my favourite photo in the country. It is a modestly framed colour snapshot, taken about thirty-five years ago, and it makes me happy every time I see it.

"Ah," says Jim, beaming, "you want to see the cruise picture."

In 1969 or 1970, somewhere back there, Jim's friends Marvin and Mary Evans invited him to join them on a weekend sailing trip. They were going to sail up to Princess Louise Inlet and view the waterfalls.

"It was a lovely weekend," says Jim. "We talked, and relaxed, and had a lovely time."

Though he seems to flourish as a bookseller, I have always had the feeling that Jim would have been just as happy had he been born as one of the characters in *The Wind in the Willows*, so I have always imagined that a weekend mucking around on a boat, any boat, anywhere, would suit Jim just fine.

"It was a lovely weekend," says Jim again, gazing at the photo fondly.

Then he points out the people in the picture and names them one by one.

"That's Marvin and Mary Evans on the left," he says. "Marvin was a Unitarian Church minister. And that is their son, I forget his name, and that is me in the blazer and sailor's cap, and that," he says ...

This is my favourite part, this is the part where he points at the tousled-haired blond boy.

"That," says Jim, still beaming, "is their son's friend, who they brought along for the trip."

He is pointing at the teenage boy in the pink golf shirt and the plaid pants in the centre of the picture.

"That," says Jim, about to deliver the coup de grace, "is Bill Gates."

Jim calls his picture "My cruise with Bill Gates."

And what does he remember of the two boys? Just this. That they stayed below deck the entire time. "They sort of irked me," says Jim. "They were sort of boring and nerdy. They weren't at all interested in any of the scenery. All they did was sit below and talk."

And what did they talk about, Jim?

"Computers," says Jim. "And how they were going to start a computer company. And all of the things they would do with it."

Jim has never seen Bill Gates since.

"He lives in Washington State," he says. "He has a huge yacht. Sometimes I see it in the harbour."

Pause.

"It is good to know that he has kept in touch with the sea."

Bill Gates is one of the world's richest men. He seems to be working hard to do good with the money he has accumulated. That is a pleasing thing to see. But what pleases me more is to visit his picture in Jim Munro's office every now and then, and be reminded that somewhere inside him is that fourteen-year-old tousled-haired boy doing what all fourteen-year-old boys should be doing: irritating adults and dreaming dreams beyond belief.

2 May 2010

ROGER WOODWARD
AND NIAGARA FALLS

When Charles Dickens saw Niagara Falls, he wrote that he seemed "to have been lifted from this earth, to be looking into Heaven."

Of all the things I know about Niagara Falls, there is one story that lifts me from this earth, one story that makes me think I have looked into heaven. It is the story of Roger Woodward, the seven-year-old boy who was, on 9 July 1960, in a small boat that capsized on the Niagara River, above the falls. Wearing nothing but a life jacket, seven-year-old Roger went over Niagara Falls—and lived.

I think about Roger Woodward every time I visit the falls. Every time I stand on the observation deck and watch the hypnotically and impossibly black water roaring over the escarpment, I wonder about him and what it could have been like to be in that water.

Last week it occurred to me that Roger Woodward would only be fifty-one years old today. And it occurred to me that if I really wanted to know what it would be like to go over the falls, I could ask him. And so I set off to find him.

It turns out Roger Woodward lives in a small town outside of Huntsville, Alabama. He is semi-retired. When I got him on the phone, I introduced myself and asked if he minded talking about his remarkable adventure. Do you remember it? I asked.

"I remember it like it was yesterday," he said. "I remember everything."

In July 1960, Roger lived in a mobile home in Niagara Falls, New York. His father worked in construction, so the family lived where the jobs were. "We were very much a blue-collar family," Roger told me. "We travelled from one place to the next, from one job to the next."

During that summer Roger's father worked at the Robert Moses power plant as a carpenter.

Roger told me that he has a sister.

"Her name is Deanne," he said. Deanne's birthday is 5 July, and to celebrate her seventeenth birthday in 1960, a family friend, Jim Honeycutt, offered to take Roger and Deanne on a boat ride. Jim had a small aluminum fishing boat. There wasn't room for Roger's mother and father.

The day of the ride, was a beautiful sunny day. Jim, Roger and Deanne set off down the Niagara River from well above the falls. Deanne was in the forward seat, Roger behind her in the middle. Jim was in the stern. There were two life jackets on board. Roger wore one of them. They tucked the other one under the front seat.

Roger remembers moving peacefully down the river in that little silver boat, remembers passing under the Grand Island Bridge—which is only a mile upriver from the falls and which many see as the last point of safety. Roger had no idea of safety points, however. He didn't even know they were anywhere near Niagara Falls. He didn't understand that one mile ahead, the river he was travelling on would tumble over the falls. It would be a day later, after he had followed the water over the edge, before he understood that.

So the little fishing boat passed under the Grand Island Bridge—the point of no return. Roger says he remembers the faces of people in other larger boats. He says he remembers thinking they looked concerned, probably because such a little boat was about to enter such a dangerous part of the river.

Ahead of them Roger saw what looked like a small white island. It was, in fact, a shoal, a small piece of land peeking up from beneath the water. It was covered with thousands of seagulls.

The little fishing boat hit the shoal. And suddenly there was no thrust from the propeller. Suddenly they were in trouble. The current was picking up and the boat had begun to drift, moving down the river, toward the falls. Jim yelled to Deanne to get her life jacket on. Then he took out the oars and tried to regain control of his boat. The water, however, was getting rough.

The average flow of the Niagara River at Queenston is greater than the Fraser, the Columbia or the Nelson rivers. They were hit by one wave, then another. The boat flipped. It happened so quickly that Deanne had only managed to get one of the straps on her life jacket done up before she hit the water. Roger had his jacket done up, but it was an adult-sized life jacket, and he didn't know how to swim. His head was throbbing—later doctors would tell him he had a concussion.

And so it was in this state, Roger, seven years old, unable to swim and wearing nothing but a giant life jacket, Deanne, with her jacket halfway done up, and Jim, with nothing at all, hit the rapids. Within seconds they were separated. Roger wouldn't see his sister for three days. He would never see Jim again.

Roger still had no idea that he was heading toward Niagara Falls or that he was tumbling through some of the most powerful rapids in the world. His head was slammed against rocks, and he was sucked under the churning water and shot back out again like he was being blown out of a whale's blowhole. He couldn't see anything.

His sister, Deanne, knew she had to swim with the current if she was going to reach the shore, and that's what she started to do. She battled the strong water and the weight of her life jacket. It felt, she would later say, as if she was swimming through peanut butter.

And just when she thought she couldn't do it anymore, just when she thought she was over, she heard a voice. The voice belonged to John Hayes. John was on land, on Goat Island, the island that separates the American Falls from the Canadian Falls. John had seen the capsized fishing boat whisk by him. John knew that if there was a boat, then there must be people too. That's when he spotted Deanne struggling to get to shore. Of all the people watching, John was the only one to take action. He ran down the riverbank to get himself in front of Deanne. Over the roar of the Niagara River, Deanne heard John's deep, strong voice calling her, "Come to me, girl," he called. "Come to me."

The falls were only a hundred feet away. His voice gave her strength. She could see John Hayes reaching out, extending his arm over the barrier that was protecting him from the water. John reaching for Deanne, and now Deanne reaching for John.

But she was moving too fast, and they missed.

Now John had to get ahead of her again. He had to get where he thought Deanne would be. And to get there, he had to outrun the powerful water that was carrying her along. He was running hard, but he was running out of land himself.

He ran down the bank and got himself in position again, this time just feet in front of the big drop. He folded his upper body over the safety barrier and reached out just as Deanne came flying by. He reached way down, and she reached way up and she caught … his thumb.

They were feet from the falls, and he had her, but only her cold, wet, slippery hand. And all she had was his thumb.

He didn't want to pull too hard because he was terrified that if he did, she might have lost her grip. He screamed for help.

John Quattrochi, a truck driver from New Jersey, ran to him. The two men reached down and pulled Deanne up by her life jacket.

The first thing Deanne did was ask, "Where's my brother?"

And that's when John looked out into the river and saw Roger Woodward's seven-year-old head bobbing up and down like a tennis ball. John leaned down and whispered in Deanne's ear. Deanne put her hands together in front of her heart.

"What did he tell her?" I asked Roger over the phone.

He said, "You need to say a little prayer for your brother. You need to say a prayer."

So Deanne put her hands together in front of her heart and

began to pray, praying for Roger, who was still being thrown around by the rapids.

Roger was panicked and terrified, unable to gain control of his own body in the paralyzing force of the river. He couldn't see anything. And he still had no idea where he was. All he knew was that he was moving fast. All he knew was that he was out of control.

If you have ever been to Niagara Falls, and stood, like I have, staring at the water, you know the Niagara River starts to flatten as it approaches the lip of the falls. Roger remembers that moment. He remembers when the rapids ended and the water smoothed.

"I was finally able to catch my breath, he said. "I was able to look around and see where I was."

What Roger saw was that he was moving swiftly toward the edge of an abyss. He remembers looking at the shore. A crowd had gathered on the riverbank. He could see them watching him. And the panic and terror he had been feeling just seconds before turned into anger. Why, he wanted to know, weren't they doing anything to help him?

Then seven-year-old Roger Woodward looked ahead. And his anger turned to submission. He was at eye level with the falls, just feet from the lip. He still had no idea it was Niagara Falls in front of him. He couldn't see the drop. He just knew he was approaching a void—a vast area of nothingness.

And that's when he realized that he was going to die.

"What did you think about?" I asked.

"I thought about my dog," he said. "And about my parents. And my toys." Roger says he remembers wondering what his parents would do with his toys when he died. He says he didn't think of heaven or hell.

"I hadn't heard of them," he said.

And then, he says, he felt at peace. That's when he dropped over the edge of Niagara Falls.

He told me when he went over, he felt as if he were floating, floating on a cloud of mist. He said it felt like he was suspended in the mist.

"There was no sensation of falling," he said. "My stomach didn't jump into my throat. And there was no smack when I hit the water, no rocks, no pain. There was nothing but mist."

The next thing he remembers is coming out of the mist and seeing the *Maid of the Mist* tour boat.

The captain that day was Clifford Keech.

One of Captain Keech's deck hands thought he spotted a child in a life jacket. And though they couldn't tell if the child was alive, Captain Keech decided to take a risk. He steered the *Maid of the Mist* off course. Roger was now in the current again—so Keech had to anticipate where the rough water was going to take him so that he could be there at the same time.

And he did. They threw a life ring to Roger, but he missed it. So they tried again.

Roger was tired and bruised. He missed it again.

On the third throw it landed right in front of the boy and Roger flopped his arms around it. They towed him up and onto the *Maid of the Mist.*

Roger remembers the nurse who looked after him at the Niagara Falls hospital. He even remembers her name, Eleanor Weaver. She brought him chocolate milk, he said. It was Eleanor who told Roger that he had gone over Niagara Falls.

And yes, he's been back to the falls. A few weeks after the accident Roger went out on the *Maid of the Mist* with Captain Keech. He said it was the first time he realized the magnitude of what had happened to him. He said he was terrified. A few months later his family went to Atlantic City. It was Roger's first time on an airplane. The pilot knew Roger was on board so, as a special treat, he flew the plane over Niagara Falls. Roger said he became hysterical. "I was afraid the plane would fall. I was afraid I'd have to do the whole thing over again."

Roger's family left Niagara a year after the accident. He didn't return to the falls again for ten years, until he was a freshman in college. He came back with his father. He says as an adult the falls didn't seem as big as they did when he was a child—not quite the monster he'd seen years before.

After college, and marriage, and kids, Roger ended up in Farmington Hills, Michigan. He and his family used to spend their holidays touring the Great Lakes on their forty-two-foot yacht. He says he didn't often think about that Saturday after-noon, so many years ago. But sometimes, when he was standing on his boat and looking down at the water of Lake Huron, he would get a pang in his stomach, knowing that the water he was floating on would flow from Huron into the St. Clair River, and from there into Lake St. Clair. And from Lake St. Clair into Lake Erie and then eventually, inevitably, become part of the violent rapids of the Niagara River on its way to and over the falls.

25 April 2004

NOTES TO SELF

MY HELLO PROBLEM

Over the years, it has been my experience that other people, my friends, my colleagues, members of my immediate family, just about everyone actually, all seem to have more under-standing of how I work than I do. They are certainly all quite willing to tell me things about me, and explain various behav-iours of mine, at the drop of a hat. And 99 percent of the time, if I am going to be honest about this, the things they say are insightful. They are able to explain, sum up and capture me in a way that I could never do.

Even complete strangers seem to know me better than I do. Just the other day, for instance, I was biking to work when I came upon a yellow light, and in a moment of intemperance, instead of slowing down, I sped up. A guy standing on the sidewalk, a complete stranger who had never met me, not once in my life, yelled out, "You idiot!" As I peeled through the intersection, and I thought about it, I had to admit it, he got *that* right.

It is as if there is a Stuart Instruction Manual out there and everyone has read it except for me. I don't even know where to get my hands on one.

I don't want to imply that I am a *complete* moron. I do know certain things about myself. I know, for instance, that if I am feeling tired or cranky, that can often mean that I am actually hungry and if I have something to eat, I will find out that I was not tired and cranky at all, just hungry. So I do have *some* insight, as they say, but most of what I seem to know about myself hovers in my brain stem, the part of the reptilian me, the place that looks after breathing and digestion. I am fairly good about that stuff, but the rest of it is pretty much a mystery. And I would be lying if I didn't tell you that I do, from time to time, wish it were otherwise.

I have heard that in psychotherapy one can experience moments of blinding insight. I have wondered what that would be like and, if I started psychotherapy myself, if I would be smart enough to have a blinding moment.

And I tell you this because just the other day I had just such a moment. A moment of startling revelation, a moment of personal clarity and self-understanding that was so stunning to me that I am still trying to process it.

I have come to call it my *Hello Problem*.

I became aware of it at the gym.

This is what happened.

I arrived at the gym and was walking toward the Men's Locker Room when Erica, who works at the gym, passed me in the hallway, coming *this* way as I was going *that*. As we passed, Erica smiled and said, "Hello, Stuart. How are you?"

Now, I happen to like Erica. Erica manages the gym, and she is a smart, funny lady. She has been helpful to me in the past and is always pleasant. But she was clearly going somewhere. And I knew I wasn't expected to stop and have a conversation with her, so I kept walking past her and as I passed I smiled. Well, I didn't just smile, I beamed. I was a picture of delight. I smiled and beamed, and I said, "Hi, Erica. How are you?" and I took about three more steps and then ... here it comes, this is the moment of insight.

I stopped dead in my tracks, and I turned and I said, "Erica?" She was almost out of sight.

"Erica?" I said. And *she* stopped, turned and said, "Yes?"

"Erica," I said, dreading the answer. "Did I just say hi to you?"

And to my horror she shook her head and said, "No, you didn't say anything."

And I realized in that instant that this was not a random moment. I realized right there and then that I do this all the time.

"Erica," I said, digging deeper, going for it. "You just said hello to me."

"Yes," she said.

"Erica," I said. "Are you *sure* I didn't say hello back?"

I already knew the answer. But I had to hear it. Because inside of me I had been the puppy dog of hello. I was sunshine and lollipops and little lambsy-diveys. Inside I smiled at Erica and said all sorts of nice things. Outside, well, the truth was otherwise. The truth was standing in front of me.

"You didn't say a thing," said Erica.

I was into it now. I went for gold. "What did that make you think?" I asked.

Erica paused and looked away. I asked again. "Erica," I said. "What did you think when I ignored you like that?"

Erica said, "Well, I thought you must have a lot on your mind."

That's what she said, but I know what she was thinking. She was thinking the same thing as that guy back at the yellow light. She was thinking, *What an idiot!*

"Erica," I said. "Does this happen often?"

I didn't have to ask. This was, after all, my moment of insight. It was all as clear as day. Suddenly I knew what went on. People smile and say hi to me all the time, and as far as they see, I respond like this. I close my mouth, frown and nod my head, the way the prime minister might nod as he passes a member of his security detail whose face he recognizes but whose name he doesn't know. Although not inside of me, understand. Inside of me there is effusiveness.

For some reason there is a malfunction, some disconnect, between my imaginary hello and, well, my actual hello.

Don't ask me why. I am not privy to that part yet. I dwell in the brain stem. Just know this: if you have ever passed me in the hall and I appeared to ignore you, it actually wasn't like that at all, and I apologize if it seemed that way.

I am not, as Erica so generously attempted to claim on my behalf, a particularly busy guy, and I certainly don't have a lot on my mind. The truth is that the guy at the yellow light got it right. I am, it turns out, an idiot.

4 October 2009

SUMMER JOBS REDUX

The summer I was seventeen I got a job at a YMCA day camp. I had had other jobs before, but this was my first real one. I don't know what made it feel more real than the others. But there you go.

The highlight of that summer was not the work, though it was work related. It came at the end of every second week, when the kids were sent home early, and we were paid, cash money, in a little brown envelope. My pal Alex Cunningham and I would take our envelopes, and our teenage selves, down the street to Murray's Family Restaurant. We would order the same lunch every time: vanilla shakes and the Hamburger Royale, which came with cheese and fries and all the fixings. And when the hamburgers came, the two of us would sit there staring at our plates like two big-time operators.

There is nothing quite like the feeling of spending money you have earned yourself.

That was the start of it for me, that summer at the Y.

The next summer, my father got me a job in the small village of Saint-Tite, Quebec. I had failed grade eleven French for the second year running. I think he decided plucking me from my anglo Montreal neighbourhood and dropping me into the heart of French Quebec would do me good. Or, more to the point, perhaps, serve me right. It was a construction job, working on a road crew who were paving the highway that ran alongside the St. Maurice River between Saint-Roch-de-Mékinac and Saint-Jean-des-Piles. When I arrived I realized, to my horror, that I was the only English-speaking person for miles. I spent an incredibly lonely couple of months in Saint-Tite.

On the weekends, when the French college boys I was living with went home to Quebec, I used to hitchhike some twenty kilometres to Grand-Mere, which was the closest place you could buy an English newspaper. One Saturday afternoon when I had picked up my *Montreal Gazette,* I took the paper into a hotel bar and sat down at a table smack in the middle of the room. It was livelier in there than you would expect for a Saturday afternoon, which I put down to the famous French joie de vivre. Trying to get into the spirit, I sprawled my feet up on the extra chair at my table, flung open my newspaper and started to read. When I spotted a waiter, I waved him over and asked for a beer. He gave me one off his tray but wouldn't take my money. I guess you pay when you're finished, I thought. And I kept reading. It was some time later, much too much later, and only when I saw the bride dance by my table, in her bridal gown, that I realized what was going on.

I had crashed a wedding, and everyone there was either too polite, or too horrified, to say anything.

One Friday, when I just had to get home to see my friends, I snuck away from work early so I could hitchhike to Trois-Rivières in time to catch the Friday train to Montreal. I didn't tell my foreman I was leaving early because I was afraid he wouldn't let me go. I left without telling anyone. When he realized I was missing, and no one could explain where or why, the foreman decided I had stumbled into the St. Maurice River and drowned. He had the river dragged and spent the rest of the weekend in horror. When I returned on Monday, he demoted me to flagboy, a hateful and tedious job.

I lasted until the middle of August. Once again I snuck away—this time in the middle of the night. I waited until my roommates were asleep and slipped out quietly. This time, I *did* leave a note. *I have to go home and write a French sup,* I wrote to the French college boys I was rooming with, *au revoir.*

I slept on a bench at the small station until the train came. It was the middle of the night. The station master signalled he wanted the train to stop by placing a red lantern at the far end of the platform. I remember the great sense of liberation I felt as the sun came up over the St. Lawrence River and I sat in the rattling dining car drinking my first-ever cup of coffee.

The few weeks had done the job. I passed my sup and got into Sir George Williams University by the skin of my teeth, and even though I have never mastered the French language the way I would have liked, that summer in Saint-Tite left me with enough fluency, and more importantly confidence, to muddle through whenever I have the opportunity. I feel grateful for those few weeks, although guilty about the cultural devastation I undoubtedly left in my wake.

The next summer, the summer of 1967, was Canada's centennial, and the summer the World's Fair, Expo 67, was mounted in Montreal. I had just finished my first year in university. As spring approached, all my new university friends were busy lining up jobs at the fair.

The theme was *Man and His World,* and my pal Nick decided to take that slogan as a personal challenge. Nick began that summer with a pledge to swing a date with a woman from each of the sixty-two participating countries. Nick, who was nothing if not well organized when it came to organizing dates, sealed the deal when he triumphantly spent the fair's final night with a flight attendant from Czechoslovakia.

While my friends spent that summer embracing the world in Montreal, I (*Qu'elle imbécile!*) decided that was the summer to head west. I took the train across the country and got myself a construction job in Calgary.

On weekends I would hitchhike to Banff where, instead of Czechoslovakian air hostesses, I spent my nights sidestepping the coyotes in the bison paddock on the edge of town. I had somehow come to the conclusion that the fence around the paddock would keep me safe from the bears. I cannot explain what made me think that camping in what amounted to a cage full of bison would be any safer than a forest full of bears, except to say that I was young and probably shouldn't have lived to be this old. Certainly not if Darwin was right about anything.

I saw a little of Expo when I got home at the end of August, although not nearly as much of the fair, or the world, as my pal Nick.

I had a number of other summer jobs over those years. I worked in a bar, as a busboy, which I left shortly after dropping a tray of drinks over a table of regular customers. In a factory assembling ski poles. And in a paint plant stacking boxes of paint onto pallets.

But my favourite summer job was my last, which was, in a pleasing sort of symmetry, working once again for the YMCA, where it all began for me.

In the summer of 1969, I got a job at Kamp Kanawana on the shores of Lake Kanawana in the Laurentian Mountains.

Kanawana is where I found my sea legs, where I was able to leave the shaky and uncertain turbulence of my adolescence behind and find the road, or, more to the point, find the where-withal to find the road, that led from adolescence to adulthood.

I was a wholly unsuccessful adolescent—a failure on the playing field and in the classroom.

I was the boy who couldn't throw the ball as well as all the other boys. Who was afraid, or unable, to study. And once you remove both academics and athletics from a boy's curriculum vitae, there is not a whole lot left to work with.

I arrived at camp with a backpack full of fears. But I found myself in a place where I felt, for the first time ever, that I fit in and had something to contribute to the greater good. That gave me confidence, and confidence is very important to the growth and development of a young person.

Kamp was my safe place.

And it is only because I found myself there, or found my best self there, that I was eventually able to find, and then follow, my heart's desire, CBC Radio.

I couldn't have done that, couldn't have tramped off into the unknown, if I hadn't had those summers at camp and, no doubt, all those other summer jobs.

I learned something at all of them.

I write about a family; what preoccupies me as a writer, however, is not the family I write about—Dave, Morley, Stephanie and Sam—but the world in which they live. And I don't mean the geopolitical world, or even the nation-state. I mean the world of the family, the neighbourhood—the safe places that foster a sense of belonging, and a sense of place, that are so enormously important to the development and preservation of healthy societies and healthy individuals.

It turns out, if you look at my work carefully, I am still working on the things that I was taught during those summers.

You wouldn't expect that a summer camp, or a construction job, or a few weeks in a bar or a paint factory would amount to much, but these things add up. And what they add up to is always bigger than you could possibly imagine.

So as another summer takes us in its warm embrace, here's to all the kids and all their summer jobs. Here's to the summer hotels and the summer camps, here's to the lifeguards and the counsellors, here's to the chambermaids and the tour guides, and to the gardeners' helpers and the landscapers.

Here's to the landscape of summer work.

Here's to waiters and waitresses. To beginnings and endings, to hellos and goodbyes. To everyone heading off into the wild blue yonder, I pray that you will learn in your summer work, as I did in mine, that work is prayer, that God is in the details and that it is a good life with much happiness to be had if you can find it. I hope, too, that you discover that a summer job, like a summer love, can be much more than you ever imagined.

17 May 2009

RUG VERSUS CHAIR

I am embroiled in a war with the rug in the room where I work. Or, rather, the wheels on my office chair and the rug are fighting, and I am sitting above them, like a Roman plebe, high up in the Colosseum as they haul away a bloodied gladiator, his bayonet and his spirit abandoned in the sand, the portal doors rise, and out comes ... the rug and chair.

It is a battle that has been fought for centuries, the battle between form and function; the chair representing function, with its plastic wheels and little levers, which allow me to adjust not only the angle of the back and the height of the seat but also the angle of the seat and the height of the back. It is a wholly unattractive chair by any standard. Big and black and ominous, the sort of chair you might see in the control room of a nuclear reactor, but since I have bought this chair, my neck and shoulders no longer ache after a day in front of my computer. It may be ugly, but it does the job.

The rug has no functional value whatsoever. It is wholly unnecessary. But it's the only aesthetic addition to a room woefully bereft of beauty. A touch of vanity, to be truthful. I bought it on an impulse after a friend turned her nose up at the ratty floor the rug now covers. Unlike the chair, the rug was cheap: $99 from a discount warehouse up the street. But it has a certain softness, and it has given me a certain satisfaction.

I sit at an L-shaped desk, and am constantly wheeling myself from one arm of the L to the other. Each time I roll, the rug rolls with me.

Well, that's not accurate, because I *come* with the same frequency as I *go,* and one would think that at the end of any day, the law of averages would dictate that the rug, while having travelled some distance, would end up more or less in position. But that's not what happens. For some reason peculiar to this rug's rugness, it only wants to move in one direction—that is to say, westward.

When I roll from the computer desk to the writing desk, my rug goes with me, but when I move back, it doesn't. Thus, at the end of every day, the rug is bunched up on one side of the room and not underfoot where it should be.

So every night before I leave my office, I roll my chair into the hall so I can put the rug back to rightness. It's an exercise that takes several minutes, and can be troublesome when you are already in your coat, and running late for dinner, as you promised not to be. After a year of this, I approach my end-of-the-day rug straightening with the same resignation with which I do the dishes—with the certain knowledge that no matter how good a job I do today, I am going to have to do it again tomorrow.

You might think that after a year I would hate this rug. Strangely, the reverse is true. Rather than resent its unruliness, I get pleasure from the few moments each day that it is straight. The last thing I do in the evening before I flick off the light is flick my eyes around the room to check if my rug is correctly squared with the walls. In the morning when I open my office door and see it lying there, I feel a flush of pride if its edges are lined up correctly.

There is no other rug I own that gives me this pleasure. I expect my other rugs to be straight and therefore get no satisfaction when they are. But this rug, my travelling rug, like an unruly child or a quarrelsome mate, is the one that pleases me, and gives me hope too, great hope, at that small moment at the start of each day, with everything in its place, that anything, anything at all, is possible.

2 February 2000

SPELLING

My grandfather, an engineer and a World War I pilot who reputedly flew his plane under London Bridge during the celebrations at the end of that war, and who everyone seems to agree was a good guy, was also, I learned recently, an atrocious speller.

"I was reading his log books," my cousin told me. "He was writing about winning something. He spelled *won*, *w-o-n-e*."

My cousin is a teacher. He seemed embarrassed about this. This was, after all, his grandfather too. I, on the other hand, was delighted.

I have never spelled *won* with both a *w* and an *e*, but I have never one a spelling bee either.

And as I consider my life as a speller, I would gladly reach for words like *ignominious*, *fiasco* and *flopperoo*, if I could spell them. (*Ed. note: you should have seen these in his draft.*) But if I want to work on my own, I am left with ~~monosillibic~~ ~~monocilabac~~ ~~mono~~ only the most simple of words. (*Ed. note: sometimes it is beyond belief.*)

I have worked on this over the years. I keep a dictionary, the Oxford, within arm's reach.

For a while I made it a habit to put a notation beside a word each time I had to check its spelling. I used to note the date as well.

I gave that up in embarrassment the seventh time I looked up *embarrassment* over a three-month period. I decided my time would be better spent working out why I needed to use the word so often.

Definitely is another word that trips me up. I want to insert the letter *a* where the second *i* is supposed to go. That is, I want, by reflex to be *definate* about things rather than *definite*. Why I seem to need to be definite so often is just another embarrassing question.

For years I paused over the word *writer*. My pen would hover over the *t*. Was there one *t* or two *t*s? I would ask myself. Over and over and over again. And when I finally got that straight, I would still trip on its gerund, writ*ing*. Surely you doubled the *t* when you added the *ing*. I often did. But not always.

Rhythm is another word that stumps me every time. Come on. There is only one vowel, and it's a *y*? Surely they meant it to be two *y*s and one *h*.

As I say, I have looked some of these words up countless times. But I have never turned to my Oxford to find the difference between *desert* or *dessert*. I am good there. One *s* in *desert*, two in *dessert*. *Dessert* has two because you always want a second helping. But how come I can remember the little trick my mother taught me for distinguishing those two words, but I can't remember if there is one *l* or two *l*s in *family*?

I know I'm not alone with these challenges. There is some comfort in that. But let's be honest, my grandfather was a pilot and an engineer, and if he wanted to spell *won* with a *w* and an *e*, what did it matter? My problem is that I am a writer or, more often, a *writter*, and *writters* really should know better. They work with werds.

1 October 2006

I AM DEEPLY SORRY

I found a note written to myself the other day that seems to say: *Apologize to L.S.*

I am not *sure* that's what it says. I have studied the note carefully, one line written on a piece of letter-sized paper. It is hard to decipher, but I wrote it. There is no doubt about that. It isn't my best handwriting. It appears I was hurried when I wrote the note. It looks like something I might have written when I was preoccupied. All I can say for certain is this: I wrote the note, and it seems to say I owe L.S. an apology.

There are several problems with this. The first, which may be an insurmountable one, is that have I no idea whosoever L.S. might be, and *why* I might owe him, or her, an apology. Although once I clearly knew *both* of these things.

And while it may be futile under the circumstance, I would, nevertheless, like to do that here and now.

I am sorry, L.S., for whatever it was I did. Or didn't.

Possibly I was late. Probably I was late. Certainly I was late. L.S., I am sorry I was late.

But it might have been more than that. Maybe I forgot something. And although I have now doubled up, and forgotten what it was that I forgot, I would like to apologize for that too. I am sorry I forgot, and I am really sorry I have forgotten whatever it is I forgot about.

I am especially sorry I have forgotten you too, L.S.

It is important you understand that although I have forgotten you right now, I'm not going to deny that (something I think should count in my favour). I could have faked it. I could have apologized and left it at that. You never would have known.

Although you seem to have vanished completely from my life, or the memory of you has vanished, it is important you understand it wasn't always so. Once you meant enough that I stopped whatever it was I was doing (exactly what that was I am no longer sure, but that is hardly important), got out a paper and pen and wrote a note, reminding myself to apologize. And yes, it might be a little late, but I am, as they say, following through, and that should count too.

Maybe one day I will wake in the middle of the night and your name will be on the tip of my tongue, where, I admit, it hasn't been for a long time, and God knows isn't right now, though I wish it were. But one night it *might* be. And if you have been waking up in the middle of the night yourself, wondering about *me*, probably thinking bad thoughts because I never apologized, I hope you will remember that actually, I did, right now.

I am sorry for being late, which, as I have already said, I am sure I was.

And I am sorry for everything I have forgotten, most importantly, your existence, but also for that thing I did back when I *hadn't* forgotten you, the thing that I never apologized for.

And while I am at it, I am sorry that I even came into your life, not for me, I didn't mind at all, I have forgotten all about, well, everything to be honest, but for you. I want you to know that when I knew you, you were on my mind, often. I used to like the way you bubbled up and distracted me, and how I used to write little notes about you, though I admit you don't bubble up as often as you used to, except for lately, and I am sorry for that too. I just wish I could remember who you are, or were, so I could forget about you again.

I am also sorry if you are two people instead of one. If you are, which just occurred to me, L *and* S, instead of L.S., I am doubly sorry to *both* of you for the misunderstanding, as *well* as everything else.

And while I am on the subject of everything else, I want to say I am sorry my handwriting is so poor, because if it were better, maybe the note would actually say something completely different, and I wouldn't be bothering you about this at all, in which case I apologize for that too.

And now that I have said that, there are a few other things I should address that don't have anything to do with you, L.S., although I can't be completely sure.

I would like to say I am sorry for the way I have been the past few weeks. Maybe you haven't noticed, but I haven't been my best self. I have been preoccupied with some things that I needn't go into right now, and that is why I might have been a little short.

I would like to apologize to the guy driving the red Tercel on Eglinton Avenue (you know who you are). You were absolutely right—that *was* an idiot thing for me to do, and I regret both it and what I said. Although you couldn't have heard my exact words, I know you got the drift of it. I want you to know I was late for an appointment, if that makes any difference. But I didn't have to respond the way I did; that wasn't helpful at all.

And to everyone I haven't phoned whom I should have phoned, I apologize. And to Bell Canada too. The cheque is in the mail. Well, it's not actually *in* the mail, but I will write a cheque tonight and will get it in the mail tomorrow. Or the day after, latest. It's as *good* as in the mail. I have the money. It's just that I have, as I said a moment ago, been a little preoccupied.

And to Mr. O'Neill, who taught me high school English, I am sorry for so much, especially for reading the Coles Notes instead of the books, but not only for that, also for the way I behaved. It was disrespectful. And it probably would have been a lot better to have said this while you were still alive. But this is the best I can do now. Maybe you can hear.

I am sorry, Mr. O'Neill, for my disrespect; and red Tercel guy, I am sorry for my rudeness; and if you are the waiter at that little Italian place where I was last week, I am sorry too (you know what I'm talking about). There are a few others while I am at it, but I really should talk to you face to face. But in case I don't get to it, I am sorry. Really. I am.

Finally, and most importantly, let me say it again, L.S., I'm sorry to you especially, for whatever it was I did, or didn't do, and for taking up your time with all this, but it has been bothering me. I needed to get it off my chest.

28 January 2007

THE JOY OF SOCKS

Looking back over fifty years of financial ineptitude, I have come to realize that I was, paradoxically, the wealthiest at that time in my life when I had the *least* amount of money.

Those would have been the years of my early teens, when my annual income was counted in the hundreds, not thousands, and came from selling Christmas, birthday and what were then called "all-purpose" cards door to door around our neighbourhood. I was alerted to the opportunity by a friend, and applied via an ad that ran regularly on the back of comic books at the time. I was moved to fill in the coupon and mail it to the Regal Greeting Card Company of Eglinton Avenue, in the faraway and mysterious City of Toronto, by my desire to own a bicycle with dropped handle-bars and more than one speed. I filled out the application with little hope of financial success. To my amazement, I made enough money selling cards, and candles that dripped multi-coloured wax, to *buy* the bike, and have enough left over that the only thing I could imagine doing with it was to put it in the bank. What more could a boy want than a bike? *That's* when I was truly wealthy, when my income exceeded my dreams.

Now, a wealthy man by many measures, not rich, not by a long shot, but with more money than I dreamed of having when I was twelve, I long for the feeling of wealth I biked around with in those spring days of my early teens, when my bank account was fat.

I still have some disposable income within reach, but I have learned enough over the years to know that using it to buy things won't make me feel rich. Possessions are more apt to saddle me with their collateral responsibilities than anoint me with a sense of wealth.

A yacht, for instance, if I could afford one, wouldn't introduce a feeling of wealth into my life. It would introduce a whole new world of worry: worry about docking fees and weather charts, the mysteries of motors and the vagaries of wind.

A sports car, if I were foolish enough to buy one, would bring with it the worry of rust and age-appropriate automobiles.

Wealth, or the sense of wealth, the sense that gave such a spring to my step when I was a young boy with $359 in the bank, cannot be bought. Or so I thought.

I thought wrong.

I have stumbled, quite by accident, on a surefire way to recapture the feeling of wealth that I had as a boy.

It is simple. It is cheap, and it can be summed up in one word: *socks*.

If you want to feel rich beyond your wildest dreams, here is what to do. Find yourself a place where they discount socks. You can get good socks for very little money if you shop around. I used to go to the McGregor factory outlet on

Spadina Avenue until it moved to the suburbs. If there is not a factory outlet near you, you can go to one of those big-box discount retailers. Unless that's against your neighbourly spirit, in which case you should go to your local clothing store and ask them what kind of break they would give you if you were to buy, say, ten, twenty, or thirty pairs of socks. The actual price isn't the most important thing. The *feeling* that you are getting a deal is. The important thing is to head to someplace where you feel like you are getting a fair deal on socks. Then you have to buy ... a lot. Of socks. The absolute number is not critical. The number will be different for different people. The critical thing is that you have to buy enough pairs of socks that you feel uncomfortable about it. You have to exceed your limit of sock comfort. You have to feel that when it comes to socks, you have gone overboard. You have, where socks are concerned, to have slipped into excess. Like those people you have read about who have way too many pairs of shoes in their closets. It has to be like that for you with socks. The feeling is the important thing here, not the actual number of pairs of socks.

In fact, it is far better that you don't actually know how many pairs of socks you buy. We are talking about socks as a substitute for wealth. John Paul Getty, a man who knew a thing or two about wealth, said if you can count your money then you are not really a rich man. So, in the strictest sense, you *shouldn't* know how many pairs of socks you have.

If you have negotiated a deal at a store where you get a discount for buying, say, twenty pairs of socks, the best way around this is to take the twenty pairs of socks to the cash and then add a few more pairs without counting.

You'll get in the spirit of this once you decide on the store. Just, as they say, do it.

Then pay for the socks. Take them home. Put them in your sock drawer without, and this is important, removing any of the packaging or labelling.

Now every morning when you get dressed, you are going to open a new pair of socks. And you are going to do that, day after day for as long as it takes. Only the very rich can afford to do something like that.

12 May 2002

ON BEAUTY

I noted with chagrin last week that the Miss Manitoba Pageant will have a blind man as part of the judging panel, part of a promise issued by Shirley Janzen, the Winkler, Manitoba–based organizer of the contest, to rate contestants on brains and not beauty.

"I'm not a supporter of beauty pageants," says Ms. Janzen.

"Neither am I," I said at lunch to the beautiful woman who brought this to my attention. "That's exactly what I think. Those contests are demeaning to women."

That's what I said, and that's what I meant, or that's what I thought I meant, until later that night when I visited a dark and private corner of my conscience, a corner I hadn't visited for a while, and I discovered that that is not what I meant at all.

I found that I am, in fact, 100 percent behind beauty, that I love beautiful things, like moonlight shimmering on the water, and ravioli pasta stuffed with sharp cheese and fresh herbs floating in a pool of virgin olive oil, and poetry (when I can understand it) and, yes, the vision of a young woman, with smooth tan skin, wearing a summer dress and a set of roller blades, weaving by on the sidewalk, her dress flapping in the wind. Truth be known, if you put a gun to my head and said I have to choose, I have to choose right now, its *brains* or *beauty*, I would say, put down the gun, I know that one, I choose *beauty* every time. Though not for my dentist, of course, or for that matter my investment dealer. Then I thought of my investment dealer, who happens to be bald and a little overweight, and who has a defective heart, and I realized that I certainly wasn't thinking of beauty when I chose him, and look where that's got me. No one would look at my portfolio these days and say *it's* a thing of beauty. In fact, my overweight broker has done nothing but deliver me capital losses for longer than I can remember. And I thought how much more palatable those losses would have been if they had been handed to me by, say, Miss Manitoba, especially if Miss Manitoba did it by moonlight, over a plate of that pasta, and she was wearing one of those little sundresses I favour, and I was looking my best too, in that grey suit I paid too much for but love nevertheless.

And you know, I bet Miss Manitoba, no matter how brainy she is or isn't, or was or will be, could have done just as well on the market these last few years as my investment dealer. All she would have needed were a few darts and that smile.

6 June 2004

THE WALL CLOCK

Recently I bought a large, round wall clock. It looked like something that might have hung on the wall of a railroad station back in the days when you needed to know the times the trains were running. I didn't need it and hadn't set off to buy one like it. I had driven a friend to a store, and was content in my role as chauffeur, until I saw the round clock and was smitten. I turned to my friend and said, "I like that clock."

"So buy it," said my friend unhelpfully.

When I got the clock home, I was overcome by the need to get it on the wall right away. The clock was ticking. Time was suddenly of the essence.

I went to the basement and fetched a ladder. I got a hammer from my toolbox. I found a little gold hook, the kind you use to hang paintings.

As I stood beside the ladder, the clock propped against the wall at my feet, I thought, *This hook is not strong enough to hold that clock.* But there were no other hooks. If I didn't use the one I had, I wouldn't be able to hang the clock until the hardware store opened the next day. I didn't have time for that.

I climbed the ladder, hammered the little gold hook into the wall, came down the ladder and picked up the clock. I hung the clock on the hook.

I had about twenty seconds to climb down the ladder, stand in the hall and admire what I had done, to see how good this clock looked on the wall, before the little hook snapped. The clock fell like a final curtain onto the tile floor and smashed at my feet. Or, more accurately, its glass face smashed at my feet. The clock kept running.

It took me about twenty minutes to pick up the last shard of glass.

The glassless clock is lying on the bed in the spare bedroom this morning, where it will, no doubt, lie until I have overnight guests and I have to face it again. It is still telling time. It has, through all this, continued to tick away, measuring out the minutes of my life and reminding me, every time I catch it out of the corner of my eye, how time inevitably defeats you, especially those times you try to hurry it along.

22 May 2005

PARKING LOT BLUES

I recently found myself standing on a street corner downtown wrestling with the growing awareness that I wasn't about to remember anytime soon where exactly I had parked my car. I'm not talking about whether I had left it on P1 or P2. It was P1; I remembered that part. The part I couldn't remember was where the parking lot was. That is when my friend Natalie arrived, right out of the blue, on her bicycle. I tried to look inconspicuous. Who, after all, wants witnesses at a moment like that? But Natalie spotted me, pulled over and said, "Hey! What are you doing?"

"Hey, Nat," I said glumly. "I can't find my car. I left it in a parking lot. Somewhere."

"That's a parking lot!" said Natalie brightly, pointing down the street. And lo and behold she was right. Not only was it a parking lot. It was *the* parking lot.

Natalie biked off, and I crossed the street, not unhappily but preoccupied by the notion that it took someone who knew absolutely nothing about where I had parked my car to find it.

It is not the first time something like this has happened. I seem to be locked in a lifelong struggle with parking lots and cars.

Most famously there was the *Episode at the Airport*. Years ago I parked my car at the Park'N Fly and I flew somewhere. I can't remember where, and that isn't important to this story. The important part is that I parked and I flew somewhere, and when I came back the folks at the Park'N Fly couldn't find my car. It was gone. They were very apologetic about this, and the way I remember it is they provided me with taxi money to get home, and when my car eventually showed up, as we all knew it would, they called me. I went and got it, and they presented me with a voucher for a couple of days free parking to make up for the inconvenience.

In fairness, it is possible that I didn't have to take a taxi at all. They might have found the car before it came to that. I might have just waited an inordinate amount of time for them to do that. The thing is, the car was missing for a while, and I left the Park'N Fly with a coupon, which I held on to for years.

When I moved, I moved the coupon with me. In truth, I did a better job keeping track of the coupon than I often do with my car. It occurred to me, however, that I was pushing my luck. It occurred to me that I should hurry up and use the coupon before I lost it. It was, after all, worth more than $100 of parking, and using it would save me about $120 in taxi fees.

As luck would have it, I was scheduled to fly to Calgary— just an overnight trip, a quick luncheon speech at a convention and then immediately home. I decided instead of taking a taxi to the airport as I usually do, I would drive, park at the Park'N Fly and use up my coupon.

I left Toronto at six o'clock on Sunday evening, arrived in Calgary around eight, had dinner in my hotel room and went right to bed. The next morning I woke early, worked out in the hotel gym, did some rewrites on a book I was working on, took a taxi to the Stampede Grounds, gave my speech, hung around and chatted with people and then hustled out to the airport. It was about three in the afternoon when I arrived.

I wasn't due to fly home until six o'clock, and I was heading to the lounge to do some more work on the book when it occurred to me I might be able to get on an earlier flight. I checked the departure board and it turned out there was one leaving in twenty-five minutes. If I could get it, I would get home at eight o'clock rather than midnight. I wasn't going to have to check luggage, so when I got home, I could jump right into a taxi without waiting for my suitcase to appear. That meant I would be home almost in time for supper. So away I went. And I made it to the gate on time, and the flight left on time, and we were actually early arriving in Toronto.

I strode through the airport feeling like the king of the world. I jumped into a taxi, and it was only when I burst through my front door that I remembered that I had driven to the airport and my car was back at the Park'N Fly.

I stood there for a moment while the enormity of this settled on me. Then I spun around and ran back into the street. I was thinking that my taxi was probably deadheading it back to the airport. I was thinking maybe if I told him my sorry story he would take me with him—maybe even for free. But all that was left of my taxi were its tail lights. Which meant I had to call another taxi and go back to the airport in *it*. The two taxis cost me the $120 I saved using the Park'N Fly coupon. And the extra trip ate up the time I saved by taking the earlier flight.

I don't want to imply this sort of thing happens to me all the time. But this sort of thing has happened before. I have driven to places, let's say to work, places that I normally walk to, and then eight hours later left work the way I am used to leaving, on foot, not remembering until the next time I need the car that the reason I can't find it is that I left it at the parking lot, ohmygoodness, that was days ago.

Once, I left a car in a parking lot and *never* returned for it. Ever. But that was mindfully. It was the first car I ever bought. A little Datsun. I paid $125 for it, and I drove it into the ground over a summer or two. It was the car I drove from Montreal to Toronto when I came, in 1976, to seek my fame and fortune. And in 1977, when I returned to Montreal having found neither, I just abandoned it.

I left it in the parking lot beside my apartment. When I came back four months later, it was gone. I figured that was better for both of us.

I have wondered recently if the parking lot woes I seem to suffer might be traced back to that moment. That there is a karmic balance being worked through—that in that first act of abandonment, I shifted the cycle of cause and effect and that I am doomed for the rest of my earthly time to wander around parking lots, stumbling, in my better moments, from P1 to P2, clicking on my key vainly, and in my darker moments, around the city, like a character from a novel by Pirandello, back and forth from parking lot to parking lot, trying to collect a car that was left behind years ago.

28 June 2009

THE NATIONAL
UMBRELLA
COLLECTIVE

I added umbrella manufacturers to my alphabetized list of cynics the other morning. The first *U* on my list. It comes right after tobacco tycoons and just before vivisectionists—the only entry for the *V*s.

I did this after purchasing a swell blue umbrella with a stylish wood handle—a leap above the telescoping, plastic-handled jobs I have always sprung for.

The clerk at the store where I purchased my umbrella gave me a knowing smile when I presented it at the cash.

"Good choice," said the clerk. And then, as if he would hardly have to mention this to someone of my good taste, "You know, of course, that this umbrella comes with a lifetime guarantee."

"If anything ever goes wrong," he continued with a little wave, which I took to mean that nothing of course *could* ever go wrong with such a fine umbrella, "just bring it in and we'll replace it."

I should mention that to get an umbrella like this you have to pay more than you, or in this case, more than I, have ever dreamed of paying for an umbrella. More, probably, than I have paid for all those folding plastic-handled jobs combined.

The impulse behind this rainy day indulgence seemed like a solid one. My idea was simple—if one bought a *good* umbrella, a stylish, *expensive* umbrella, one could expect oneself to remain moderately mindful of it and, consequently, less likely to leave it in a taxi, or slung over a chair in a café, park bench, subway—go ahead, take your pick.

One *might* think that.

Until one inevitably does forget it somewhere on, I will add here, risking a descent into yet unplumbed depths of self-loathing, the very first day one takes it to work; and that is when one, oh let's be honest here, that's when *I* was struck by this notion that the whole business of guaranteeing an umbrella against mechanical defects is, as I mentioned a moment ago, a cynical business. I can't think of anyone I know who has held on to an umbrella long enough for any sort of mechanical defect to present itself, let alone long enough to use it for, sigh, a rainy day.

I should mention that I have, over the years, not been entirely unlucky in the umbrella game. One *assumes* it should be a zero sum game; one *assumes* there must be some force or being at work in the cosmos, some sort of umbrella fairy whose job it is to ensure that the balance of umbrellas lost and umbrellas found works out more or less evenly. And I *have* found the odd umbrella these past fifty-odd years.

But not nearly as many, it seems to me, as I have left behind me for *others* to find; and when I asked around the other day, I found that everyone I asked feels that way too.

So unless there is someone out there, or a group of someones out there, who is, or are, unusually lucky in this business, I have to assume most of us lose more umbrellas than we find, a subject worthy of wondering about, which I will leave for others to ponder.

What I would like to put forward is that perhaps the time has arrived to add the umbrella to the social safety net.

If we lose our health, we have medicare. If we lose our job, there is employment insurance. When we lose our youth, there is the old age pension. Why shouldn't there be help when we lose our umbrellas? Which just like health, wealth and youthfulness we all know we are bound to lose one day, no matter how mindful we are.

I would like to propose The National Umbrella Collective.

Because even in the unlikely event you are one of those someones who find more umbrellas than you lose, it can't be easy on you, it can't be all sunshine and roses, because I have, as I said, found the odd umbrella and I know what happens.

There is an initial swell of good feeling, as if finally life's balance has begun to tip your way, and if it keeps tipping maybe even stock trades and real estate investments might work out, or at least break even.

But then the wave of doubt hits. What happens, you wonder, if it starts to rain? What happens if you put your new umbrella up and the original owner sloshes by, shoulders hunched, and recognizes it? What happens then?

Thus, my proposal.

Tomorrow morning, whatever the weather, take your umbrella with you when you leave your house. When you get where you are going, leave your umbrella behind—leave it on the backseat of the taxi, or propped on the seat of the subway, or up against a newspaper box on the street outside your office. You don't want to tote it around all day, and let's face it, if you did, you'd eventually leave it somewhere anyway, so leave it somewhere obvious, where it will wait for the next rainy day guy who forgets his—a guy who might even be you.

If we all did this, if we all agreed to agree on the matter of public umbrellas, we could all be a little bit happier on rainy days.

23 October 2005

BOB DYLAN'S
PHONE NUMBER

I have a notebook with Bob Dylan's home phone number in it. I know it's authentic because I got the number from Pete Seeger. Pete didn't actually *give* me the number. He enabled me. He left me alone with his phone book, which was open at the *D*s at the time (I don't remember, but that would be the *charitable* explanation). It is possible that the phone book was closed when I picked it up.

This was long ago and far away, although I don't mean to imply I wouldn't, if placed in the same situation today, flip through Pete's phone book. The point of this, or part of the point, is that I have had Bob Dylan's home number for a long time. More than twenty-five years.

Here's how I got it. I was working on a profile of Pete Seeger for the CBC Radio show *Sunday Morning*. Pete had invited me down to his house on the Hudson River, where, at eighty-seven, he lives today, in case you were wondering. I had flown down to New York City, rented a car and driven up the Hudson to the town of Beacon. As I recall, I slept on a couch on Pete's sun porch.

Although he had graciously invited me into his home, Pete and I were having trouble with each other. Ever modest, he was doing his best to avoid talking about himself. Every time I suggested bringing out my tape recorder, Pete would suggest something else.

"Let's go down to see the boat," he said. Pete was and still is involved with the sailing sloop *Clearwater* and a project to draw attention to the fragile health of the Hudson River.

"Let's go visit a school," he said another morning. And off we went to a local elementary school, where Pete had been asked to drop by and sing a few songs.

When I finally sat him down and turned on my tape recorder, all Pete would talk about was Woody Guthrie.

When he finished that, he sent me back to New York City to talk to Woody's wife, Marjorie, and his manager, Harold Levanthol.

After a couple of days of this toing and froing, I was beginning to panic. Finally, in desperation, I told Pete we *had* to do the interview.

"Okay," said Pete, "You go into the bedroom, and I will be there in a second."

That is how I came to be sitting on Pete Seeger's bed staring at his phone book, which was lying there on the bed in front of me, either open at the *D*s or not.

In any case, pretty soon it was, and I remember, as if it were yesterday, staring at the handwritten notation that read, *Bob Dylan (Home) Malibu.*

I knew this piece of information wasn't meant for me, and I could have closed the book. I did, but I wrote the number down first, and soon after I did, Pete came in the bedroom. We did the interview, I wrote and edited the piece, it went on the radio, and when it was all over, well, I had Bob Dylan's home phone number.

Now, once you possess something like that you have more than the number, you have a problem. What are you going to do with it? I considered a number of possibilities. I could call Bob Dylan, and when he answered, I could hang up. Or I could ask for "Larry." Or, better, "Pete," which would be sort of clever.

If I did any of those things Bob Dylan would have to engage me in conversation. He would have to tell me I had the wrong number, and I could say thanks and hang up, but I would have had a conversation with Bob Dylan. Of course I could also try to do that—have a *real* conversation with him, I mean.

I knew that if I did *any* of these things, especially the latter, Bob would probably have his phone number changed and then, well, then I would have caused problems for him, something I didn't really want to do, but more importantly I wouldn't have his phone number anymore, would I?

I decided that *having* his phone number, and therefore possessing something no one else I know possesses—that is, the *possibility* of phoning Bob Dylan—was far better than any version of a real call that I could imagine.

So I never called.

I have the phone number in front of me right now, and even though a lot of water has gone under the bridge, for Bob and me, even though it is pretty clear neither of us are going to be *forever young*, and even though he may have changed the number many times since that afternoon, maybe he hasn't.

And because I haven't called, and because I never will, that possibility still exists today, and will tomorrow too—the possibility that one lonely night I could call him, and we could talk, and if we did, who knows? The possibility exists that we might even have something to say to each other.

Just having it keeps that little dream alive and provides me, whenever I think about it, with a sense of quiet satisfaction.

I have Bob Dylan's phone number, and because I do, my little world shines brighter.

25 March 2007

THE GIRL IN THE GREEN DRESS

I went to an all boys' school. I was painfully shy and self-conscious, especially around girls. So I never had a girlfriend. Not even close. When everyone else was falling in love and kissing each other, I wasn't kissing anyone.

In grade ten there was a school dance. It was held on a Friday evening in October. I was, maybe, fifteen years old. I wanted to go to the dance. I bought a ticket. And then I came face to face with the *next* step. I needed a date. When you go to an all boys' school, you can't show up at a dance without a date. If everyone did that, there would be no one to dance with. Only a loser would go alone. Probably no one ever had gone alone in the history of the school. I wasn't about to be the first.

I had to find a girl to go with. And I didn't have a hope of doing that.

I could have asked my friend Marilyn. She was sort of the girl next door—a pal who had a cottage up at the lake. But I didn't ask her. I don't mean disrespect, but I didn't want to go with a pal. I wanted romance. Instead of doing something about that, I waited for something to happen. Of course, nothing did.

Maybe in some spoony moment I phoned a girl, intending to ask her to come with me. I seem to remember doing that, but probably her mother answered and I hung up. I used to do that from time to time, mostly from phone booths so no one in my family could be party to my ineptitude. Or, perhaps, my desire. Phoning a girl was the scariest thing in the world. Rejection, the likely outcome, seemed so certain and so horrible that just dialing the numbers took hours of preparation.

So on the Friday night of the dance when my dad told me he would drive me, and I said that would be okay, I had to come up with a story that would explain my missing date. I told him I had arranged to meet her at the dance.

He dropped me at the front door of my school. I hung around outside, waiting for him to leave. When he was out of sight, I took off. I had a plan.

There was that same night a teen dance at a nearby community centre that I had read about in a local paper. My plan was to go to that dance, find a girl there and ask her to come to the school dance with me.

I was desperate. I couldn't go alone.

I got to the community centre and scoped the room. All of the girls were wearing jeans. That was a deal breaker. I couldn't take a girl in jeans to my school dance. It was a semi-formal. There was one girl wearing a dress, however. I waited for a slow song and asked the girl in the dress to dance with me. She agreed. While we danced I told her about the dance at my school. *Want to go with me?* I asked. As I write this I am thinking it could sound kind of cool. I go to one dance, pick up a girl and take her to another. I want you to understand that I was frantic. Cool was nowhere on the radar.

Surprisingly, the girl agreed. I remember her dress, the one that made me choose her. It was green. But that's *all* I remember. I certainly don't remember her name. But if this sounds vaguely familiar, if you are the girl in the green dress, I would love to talk to you again. I would love to say thanks.

But that is not why I still think of that night. What I think about is this: as we walked from that community dance to the dance at my school, I made the girl in the green dress promise she wouldn't tell anyone at the dance where we had met.

"I'm going to tell everyone that I know you from my cottage," I said.

I can't remember how I explained this to her. I'm sure I didn't tell her the truth. The truth was I didn't want anyone to know I was a desperate loser who had to find his date at a local community centre at the last minute.

So we went to my school dance, and the only other thing I remember from the rest of that night is that I walked the girl in the green dress home. I had never kissed a girl before, and I remember as we came upon her house, I began to wonder if this was going to be the night I was finally going to get kissed. It wasn't.

And here is why I am telling you all this. Here is what I want to know. Why all those lies? If I had told my buddy Mike that I didn't have a date the week before the dance, I know he would have fixed me up. He might even have offered anyway. I seem to have a vague memory of that happening. But I didn't let him.

And why didn't I tell my dad? What a great father-and-son talk that could have been. *Hey, Dad, can I tell you something?*

And while I was walking that girl in the green dress home, why didn't I tell her I had never kissed a girl before, and that I really wanted to kiss her goodnight. Why didn't I tell her I was nervous, and would do it if I knew how, but I didn't know how. Why didn't I tell her I was afraid? How adorable would that have been? Who could have resisted that? The simple truth would have got me my heart's desire.

I have wondered about that over the years. It has taken me an awful long time to learn that simple lesson. I am getting better at it these days. Speaking from my heart and saying what I really and deeply feel. I try to do it especially when I am feeling afraid and vulnerable because I have learned that the only thing that ever really serves you is the truth, especially when it's hard and difficult.

I try to remember that if I had spoken my heart, that girl in the green dress probably would have kissed me that October night, the wind blowing the leaves, the moonlight suddenly so much softer.

1 October 2008

THE DESK LAMP

I bought a lamp at a craft show. It is a small table lamp, less than a foot high. It has an antique brass stand and a shade made of milky glass. It is too low to the ground, or, to be more precise, to the desk where I work, to shed any light and too reticent about the light-shedding business in any case—it tends to "glow" rather than illuminate, the light too soft to be of any help other than to the mood.

Yet in the mood-setting business, my little lamp is a prince among lamps. A day doesn't pass without it brightening my mood.

I turn it on every morning when I sit down to set about my work (which given the abundance of light in my office in the morning is akin to lighting a campfire on a summer afternoon). And maybe it's this essentially unessential quality, above its graceful milky-ness and its warm yellowness, that makes my little lamp so appealing.

As I sit at my desk, day in and day out, answering my phone, paying my bills and scribbling away in between, I know that my lamp and I share this fundamental fact: neither of us is really necessary in this big wide world of light. But bidden, or unbidden, we are here nevertheless. Here by the grace of some big unknown thing. And while we are here, we will shine when we are called to, and do our best to shine as brightly as we can, shining away until the dark morning when someone will forget to turn us on.

6 February 2005